THE VIENNA CIRCLE

THE VIENNA CIRCLE

The Origin of Neo-Positivism
A chapter in the history of recent philosophy

By
VICTOR KRAFT
Professor of Philosophy at the University of Vienna

PHILOSOPHICAL LIBRARY
NEW YORK

Translated from the German "Der Wiener Kreis"

By

ARTHUR PAP

PRINTED IN THE UNITED STATES OF AMERICA

INTRODUCTION

The Vienna Circle constituted (together with the society for empirical philosophy in Berlin) a point of departure for an international philosophical movement which led to a rebirth and reformation of positivism and empiricism. Neo-positivism stands in the foreground of contemporary philosophy, especially in the anglo-saxon and scandinavian countries. It may safely be said to be the most significant of serious philosophical movements in the period between the two world-wars. But it is just in the German cultural domain that the work of the Vienna Circle has been unconditionally rejected—if it has been at all taken notice of. Indeed, acquaintance with the work of the Vienna Circle has been and still is very scant in Germany. It is but the beginnings that are known. This is evidenced by the fact that Gerhart Lehmann, in his history of "Contemporary German Philosophy", which was published as recently as 1943, mentions only Carnap, and gives, indeed, an enumeration of his early writings, his doctoral dissertation, his essay on "Eigentliche und uneigentliche Begriffe" of 1927, his "Logische Aufbau der Welt" and the "Scheinprobleme" of 1928 as well as the "Grundriss der Logistik" of 1929, but fails to mention any of his later publications, which are of such importance. And even the works referred to are entirely misinterpreted, their main points being missed entirely. Likewise Del Negro, whose "Geschichte der deutschen Philosophie der Gegenwart" appeared but one year earlier, still refers to the "Logische Aufbau" as the most important publication of the school. None of the numerous publications which came out subsequently, the articles in the eight volumes of "Erkenntnis", Carnap's "Logical Syntax of Language", Schlick's "Gesammelte Aufsaetze", documenting the development and progress of the Vienna Circle, were taken notice of. These publications, and in fact the entire movement, were afterwards played down and suppressed in the intellectual climate of national socialism. Even in the recent survey of "Contemporary European Philosophy" by Bochenski (1947), which is a good book on the whole and contains a far better discussion of neo-positivism and the Vienna Circle than the above mentioned books, there are slight inadequacies and the discussion is all too brief.

More thorough analyses of the work of the Vienna Circle are to be found mainly in writings outside of Germany. We have here above all the large expert monograph by J. R. Weinberg "An Examination of Logical Positivism", London, 1936, which nevertheless refers primarily to the earlier phase, dominated by Wittgenstein. A penetrating analysis is further contained in the excellent discussion of neo-positivism by G. H. von Wright, "Den logiska Empirismen", Helsingfors, 1943; but as it is written in Swedish, it is difficult for the general reader to get access to it. The remaining expositions outside of Germany date partly from the early period of the Vienna Circle, like Kaila's excellent critical essay "Der logische Neupositivismus", published as early as 1930, and the monograph, adequate at the time but of course by now outdated, "Der logische Positivismus", by Petzaell, 1931, as well as the same author's critique of protocol sentences

"Zum Methodenproblem der Erkenntnisforschung",
1935. And partly they consist in very brief digests like
those by Vouillemin, "La logique de la science et l'école
de Vienne", 1935, and by C.W. Morris, "Logical Positivism, Pragmatism and Scientific Empiricism", 1937. (The
article by Blumberg and Feigl has unfortunately remained inaccessible to me, in spite of my efforts). Among
expositions abroad of the doctrines of the Vienna Circle,
the book "Language, Truth and Logic", by A.J. Ayer
(1938; 2nd edition 1946), should also be mentioned.

For these reasons, I thought it would serve a good
purpose to present a synoptic discussion of the philosophical achievements, problems and conclusions of the
Vienna Circle; not just in order to save them from oblivion, but above all in order to put the fundamental ideas
of this movement before the eyes of contemporary German philosophers, who are not sufficiently familiar with
them.

The days of the Vienna Circle are gone—at least in
Vienna. Its work, in which I myself participated, is finished, and that is why my exposition extends only to the
time of the Circle's dissolution, in 1938. Indeed, it would
have been impossible anyway to keep sufficiently in-
formed of publications abroad by former members of the
Circle as well as publications referring to the Vienna
Circle which have come out in the meantime, considering
the state of isolation from foreign countries which the
second world war brought with itself. Hence it was not
possible to take such recent literature into account, Carnap's recent works excepted.

In judging the work of the Vienna Circle one should
not lose sight of the fact that it has not been finished but
was suddenly disrupted. Many extreme oversimplifica-

tions and radicalisms can be explained as early stages of an unfinished development. The fact that views held in the Circle have changed repeatedly, as is illustrated by Carnap's abandonment of the onesidedly syntactic point of view, indicates that surely more mature solutions would have been arrived at in the Vienna Circle if only the work could have been continued. It would, indeed, be easy to throw a completely different light on their achievements than is done in the following, if one wished to emphasize extreme formulations and consequences. But thus injustice would be done to the Vienna Circle. The great positive significance of their work is beyond doubt. Not that I would be willing to defend the views of the Circle without reservations; as a matter of fact, I have inserted critical remarks on some fundamental points here and there into my exposition. Yet, the manner in which the Vienna Circle strove to clarify the foundations of knowledge penetratingly and comprehensively, and the degree of clarity and rigor with which this task was actually accomplished, are unparalleled in recent German philosophy. There is much to be learned from the Vienna Circle even by those who do not share its point of view.

V. Kraft

Vienna, March, 1950

PREFACE

The movement initiated by the Vienna Circle has produced no echo in the German speaking countries, but it has been received and promoted abroad, in England and in the Scandinavian countries and particularly in the United States where it has undergone a lively development. The publication of an English translation of my description of the origin of this movement is, therefore, justifiable and an event to be grateful for. My book contains a survey over the problems, as well as their attempted solutions, which constituted the point of departure, and it will be easier to grasp the foundations and the uniting bond of the various emanations and further developments from this platform. It is not only to the Philosophical Library, but especially to Professor Pap, who carried the translation through with great care and conscientiousness, that I owe thanks for making my book, and therewith the work of the Vienna Circle, accessible to the vast domain of the anglo-saxon countries. The difficult task of hitting on the corresponding technical terms and of preserving exactly the meanings of the translated sentences, presupposes intimate familiarity with the material, subtle in parts, and accordingly it took as expert a person as Professor Pap to accomplish this task. Thanks to his efforts, several passages have even received a more precise formulation in the English translation — thus it is only through him that the terminological distinction between "sentence" and "proposition" has been consistently observed —, and he made valuable additions in the form of footnotes.

My book covers only the original work of the Vienna Circle which was disrupted by the outbreak of the second world war. It would be extremely desirable if someone were to write a history of the further development of the movement initiated by the Vienna Circle up to the present time. It would be far easier to do this in the United States than in Europe, since the movement is centered in the United States while it is far more difficult to survey the new literature from a distance. It is unlikely that I myself would still be able to undertake this task.

VICTOR KRAFT

Vienna, May 1952

CONTENTS

CONTENTS

PART ONE

THE HISTORY OF THE VIENNA CIRCLE

THE HISTORY OF THE VIENNA CIRCLE[1]

THE UNIVERSITY OF VIENNA has had a chair for philosophy of the inductive sciences since 1895; it was first instituted for Ernst Mach who held it until 1901. After him it was taken over by L. Boltzmann (from 1902 until 1906), and still later Adolf Stoehr, the original thinker, occupied it. Thus there has existed a long tradition of empiricist philosophy in Vienna, concerned primarily with the natural sciences. But even before that time empiricist tendencies had in a sense asserted themselves through Franz Brentano. Theodor Gomperz and Jodl had represented anti-metaphysical philosophy, and in 1922 the chair for philosophy of the inductive sciences was offered to Moritz Schlick. He had, not unlike his predecessors, come to philosophy from physics. His doctoral dissertation, written under Planck, was on the topic of light-reflection in non-homogeneous media, and through his monograph "Space and Time in Contemporary Physics", 1917, he became the first philosophical interpreter of the theory of relativity. He entertained personal contacts with leading men in the exact sciences, such as Planck, Einstein and Hilbert. But what distinguished him from his predecessors, Mach as well as Boltzmann, was his intimate knowledge of philosophy.

Soon a circle formed itself around Schlick in Vienna, consisting not only of students but also of intellectuals interested in philosophy. It contained the most advanced students of his—among them Fr. Waismann was outstanding—, but also accomplished Ph.D.'s, like Neurath, E. Zilsel, H. Feigl, B. v. Juhos, H. Neider, further some of his closer or remoter colleagues, viz. lecturers R. Carnap, V. Kraft, F. Kaufmann, and by no means just "pure" philosophers, but likewise philosophically interested mathematicians: Professor H. Hahn and lecturers Menger, Radakovic and Goedel. The indicated composition of the circle was responsible for an unusually high level of discussion. The mathematical representation—Carnap, Waismann, Zilsel, Neurath, Kaufmann too were mathematically competent—reinforced the tendency towards logical rigor and precision. In shorter and longer meetings logical and epistemological problems were discussed, and thanks to the background and original analyses of the leading participants[2]—primarily Schlick, Carnap, Neurath, Waismann, Hahn, Zilsel—a good many positive results were achieved. What went on was cooperative, constructive analysis, not mere reception of a teacher's doctrines. Schlick was by no means the one and only leading figure. Many influential suggestions came from Wittgenstein, though the latter was never personally present. They were transmitted by Schlick and Waismann who were in personal contact with Wittgenstein, at that time in Vienna. Thus Wittgenstein's influence extended far beyond the influence exercised by his Tractatus Logico-Philosophicus.[3] The cooperative work of the Vienna Circle resulted in such rapid progress as usually occurs only in the special sciences. Naturally, such a rapid development involved repeated changes of views, and it was to be expected that several of the original, oversimplified doctrines would in time be superseded.

In 1929 Schlick was called to Bonn, but after some

4

hesitation he refused. In the spring and summer of the same year he went to Stanford University, California, as visiting professor. It was during this period when they faced first the possibility of losing him and then his prolonged absence, that the members of the Circle became conscious of the fact that they formed an intellectual community *sui generis,* an independent philosophical group. The meeting of the German Physical Society and the German Mathematical Association, at Prague in the middle of September of the same year, was the external occasion for presenting themselves as an independent group organizing concurrently a congress for epistemology of the exact sciences, jointly with the society for empirical philosophy in Berlin, with such members as Fr. Kraus, H. Reichenbach, A. Herzberg, A. v. Parseval, W. Dubislav, K. Grelling. At the same time a small programmatic pamphlet "Wissenschaftliche Weltauffassung. Der Wiener Kreis" was published, written by Carnap, Hahn and Neurath; it briefly described the history and membership, the orientation and the goals of the circle. The pamphlet was dedicated to Schlick and handed to him when he returned to Vienna in October 1929, "as an expression of gratitude and joy over his return to Vienna", as it said expressly in the preface. Thus the "Vienna Circle" entered publicity.

This new phase also manifested itself in the Circle's adoption of a special organ of publication: the periodical "Annalen der Philosophie" was taken over in 1930 by Carnap and Reichenbach and continued under the name "Erkenntnis". The Circle found a further means of publication in the small monographs "Veroeffentlichungen des Vereines Ernst Mach", edited by the society "Ernst Mach" which was founded in 1928 by several members of the Circle with a tendency towards popularisation;[4] further the series "Einheitswissenschaft", edited by Neurath, 1934.

From then on the "Vienna Circle" became rapidly known to an ever expanding public. In September 1930 they organized, again jointly with the Berlin group for empirical philosophy, a congress for epistemology of the exact sciences at Koenigsberg, in connection with the German congress of physicists and mathematicians; the topic was foundation problems in mathematics and quantum-mechanics.[5]

Carnap's invitation to the faculty of natural science at the University of Prague, as assistant professor, meant indeed a distinct loss for the Vienna Circle; however, Carnap now formed together with Philip Frank, the professor of physics, a branch of the "Vienna Circle" in Prague. Both groups made contacts with congenial thinkers abroad, with Joergensen, professor of philosophy at Copenhagen, with Rougier, at that time professor at Besançon and Kairo, with Morris, university professor at Chicago, with Miss Stebbing, university professor in London, and others. Personal intercourse was also established with the logistic schools in Warsaw and Lemberg.[6] Out of all these contacts grew an international congress of scientific philosophy, organized in 1934 at a preliminary meeting in Prague by Rougier, Reichenbach, Carnap, Frank and Neurath, and staged in September 1935 at Paris in the halls of the Sorbonne.[7] The congress was promoted by the French government and by international scientific institutes in Paris; Russell and Enriques made opening speeches, and about 170 members from more than 20 countries participated; from Germany only Professor Scholz, Muenster, was present besides the Berlin group. It was a great success. If the Vienna Circle's outlook still met vehement opposition at the Prague meeting of 1929, it was now largely shared. Enriques and General Vouillemin only cautioned against dogmatism and neoscholasticism, Morris against onesidedness and Reichenbach against the tendency to condemn something as metaphysics prematurely; some members were critical of some specific views. Upon a suggestion of Carnap's a committee for international unification of logical symbolism, first for the German terminology, was formed; the congress also declared its readiness to promote and cooperate with the international encyclopedia of unified science, recommended by Neurath.[8]

Immediately the following year, in July 1936, a second international congress "for unity of science" was held in Copenhagen, dedicated especially to the problem of causality, with particular attention to quantum-physics and biology.[9] Close to 100 members, from most European countries and especially many from the United States, participated; N. Bohr gave the first paper. In his address, Joergensen emphasized that the initiative for this and the preceding congresses had come from the "Vienna Circle", and that the fundamental ideas of the new philosophical movement must be credited to the latter. The following year, in July 1937, a third congress for unity of science was held again in Paris, at the Sorbonne, for the purpose of discussing the planned encyclopedia.[10] And again a year later, in July 1938, a fourth congress for unity of science took place at Cambridge, dealing with the language of science.[11] G. E. Moore gave the opening address, and the attendance was again international. The last of these congresses was held in the United States, in September 1939, at Cambridge, Massachusetts. Then the

war put an end to them. It was a splendid rise. The
Vienna Circle had turned into an international philosophical movement, into Neo-Positivism or Neo-Empir-
icism.

But in the meantime the Vienna Circle itself had
suffered painful losses. In 1931 Feigl accepted a pro-
fessorship at the University of Iowa, and was subsequently called to the University of Minnesota. In 1934 Professor Hahn died unexpectedly. In 1936 Carnap, having
been awarded an honorary doctor's degree by Harvard
University, went to the United States where he accepted
a position at the University of Chicago.[12] And during the
same year the Circle was dealt its heaviest blow: Professor Schlick was shot at the University by a mentally
deranged former student. It was a loss beyond repair,
to have Schlick thus torn away from his fruitful work and
to have his further development cut off, with a good many
projects left behind unfinished. Now the meetings of the
Circle were discontinued, and after the forced annexa-
tion of Austria by Germany in 1938 the organization dissolved completely. Its members were dissipated into all
parts of the world. Waismann and Neurath went to England, where Waismann became a university professor,
first at Cambridge and then at Oxford, and where Neurath died in 1946; Zilsel and Kaufmann went to the
United States where Zilsel died in 1943; Menger and
Goedel had already followed up invitations to that country. "Erkenntnis" moved in 1938 from Leipzig to den
Haag, where it assumed in volume 8 the title "The
Journal of Unified Science (Erkenntnis)", but had to
discontinue publication, in 1940, because of the war.
The sale of publications by the Vienna Circle was prohibited, for political reasons, because there were some

8

Jews among its members and because the activity of the society "Ernst Mach" was regarded as "subversive".

There was no more Vienna Circle in Vienna. But its viewpoint was represented abroad where it gained more and more ground; above all in the United States where there existed already a parallel movement,[13] represented by Morris, Langford, Lewis, Bridgman, Nagel, where Reichenbach and R. v. Mises have found a home, and where at the present time Carnap in Chicago and Feigl in Minnesota, Bergmann in Iowa and Hempel at Yale University continue the work. In England, the country where, after all, Russell dwells as an ancestor of the entire movement, the Vienna Circle is perpetuated through Waismann at Oxford and through Ayer—as well as through Popper, in essentials—at the University of London; at the same university Miss Stebbing (deceased 1943) represented a similar point of view.[14] Dr. Popper, it is true, never participated in the meetings of the Vienna Circle, but he stood in personal intellectual contact with several members (Carnap, Feigl, Kraft). The work of the Vienna Circle has been continued in a most remarkable way in Finland, through Kaila, who like Ayer had for some time personally participated in the Circle's evening sessions, and through G. H. v. Wright, Kaila's former student and colleague at the University of Helsinki, now Professor at Cambridge. Dr. H. A. Lindemann, also a member of the Vienna Circle, returned to Buenos Aires where he had been living before, and where he now exercises his literary activity. Dr. Tscha Hung, who also was a member of the Vienna Circle, is now professor at the University of Peiping, before at the University of Wuhan, Wuchang, China. Naturally, the erstwhile members of the Vienna Circle have not stayed

9

on their platform but have developed further and in part superseded their original views.

Philosophers close to the Vienna Circle are also Professor Joergensen in Copenhagen and Professor Dürr in Zürich, Professor Rougier, General Vouillemin, M. Boll and others in France. Connections with the Vienna Circle have been established also in places where at least partly similar ideas dominate, such as the empiricist school in Uppsala and Professor Tegen at Lund,[15] the logistic schools at Goettingen and Muenster, at Warsaw and Lemberg;[16] the latter two, however, have been dissolved by the war just like the Vienna Circle.

In Germany alone the ideas of the Vienna Circle have not been propagated. While Russell, for example, mixes his criticism with genuine admiration,[17] and even more critical people have not denied the significance of these ideas,[18] they have here, if not completely ignored, been repudiated firmly and contemptuously.[19] In the essay "L'école de Vienne et la philosophie traditionelle",[20] Schlick writes of the complaints against the Vienna Circle: "Frequently the Vienna School is accused of consisting, not of philosophers, but of enemies of philosophy. The teachings of this school, they say, contribute nothing to the development and progress of philosophy, but on the contrary to its dissolution". But one could not talk that way unless one equated philosophy with metaphysics. Yet, surely the rejection of metaphysics is not original with the Vienna Circle.[21] The understanding words which Schlick finds, in the same essay, for historical philosophy prove that the accusation of contempt for philosophy is unfounded:[22] "The 'anti-metaphysicians' are often unjust to traditional philosophy when they declare that the latter is nothing but a collection of pseudo-

10

problems. I think, on the contrary, that we have every reason to be proud of the fact that our ideas are the result of a long historical development of the human mind". "We shall show historical understanding for the systems of the past, their dogmas do not irritate us any more; we may admire with a clear conscience the grand epochs of a human species which exhibits a profound drive towards truth, in its inquiries and in its errors alike". One should not judge the Vienna Circle's attitude towards traditional philosophy by the expressions of its radical members alone. Indeed, he for whom philosophy is the expression of individual wisdom about life and world, a subjective interpretation of life and the world or for whom it is the search for the speculative construction of an explanation, concealed and unknowable outside of philosophy, of the world, or for a sort of conceptual world-poetry—he, indeed, cannot but look upon philosophy as interpreted by the Vienna Circle as an impoverishment. For it excludes everything that is not attainable by scientific method. But in this way alone is it possible to get beyond its subjective diversity and instability, in this way alone can we expect to reach universal validity and lasting results.

PART TWO

THE WORK OF THE VIENNA CIRCLE

THE WORK OF THE VIENNA CIRCLE

THE COMPOSITION of the Vienna Circle made it inevitable that there would be no such uniformity of views as might be expected in a mere circle of disciples who simply adopt the teacher's opinion. For, after all, at least the leading members were independent thinkers. There was a radical wing, led by Neurath, and joined by Hahn and also by Carnap quite often, which had, just because of its radicalism, frequently a stimulating and at times a seductive influence, and there was a more moderate faction to which Schlick belonged. On matters of detail, there were many differences, some of them touched upon in Schlick's essay "L'école de Vienne . . ."[1] Also attitudes towards the theses of Wittgenstein were divergent, and neither was there unanimity in the theory of probability. But there was agreement about fundamental matters. There was one common tenet: that philosophy ought to be scientific. The rigorous requirements of scientific thinking were postulated for philosophy. Unambiguous clarity, logical rigor and cogent argument are as indispensable to philosophy as to the other sciences. There is no place in philosophy for dogmatic assertions and untestable speculations, such as still nowadays abound in philosophy. Opposition to all dogmatic-speculative metaphysics was implicit in these postulates. Metaphysics was to be completely eliminated, and thus the Vienna Circle was tied to positivism.

Over and above this general orientation, however,

15

there was far-reaching agreement about basic views. The outlook was empiricism, as represented by Russell, which entailed the rejection of apriorism. There cannot be synthetic a priori judgments in the Kantian sense. Statements about reality can be valid only on the basis of experience. The new logic, as developed by Whitehead and Russell more than a decade before that time, contributed further to a common ground. A common starting-point was provided also by the philosophy of language which Ludwig Wittgenstein, proceeding in his *Tractatus logico-philosophicus* (1922) [2] from the work of Russell and Whitehead, had developed. It was through critical examination of his ideas, leading partly to their further development, partly to their transformation, partly to their abandonment, that the work of the Vienna Circle unfolded to a great extent.

Accordingly attention was given primarily to logical, epistemological and semantic questions; but likewise problems of a scientific picture of the world were dealt with. Thanks to such broad unanimity it was never necessary to spend much time and effort on securing a common basis of discussion, and the specific problems could be tackled immediately. This was the reason for the unusual fertility of this cooperative enterprise.

A. LOGIC AND LANGUAGE

I. *Logic and Mathematics*

The new logic had special significance for the Vienna Circle, as is shown also by the labels the philosophy of the Vienna Circle has been given: "logistic neo-positivism", or "logical empiricism".[3]

Since the latter half of the 19th century logic has

been transformed and expanded in a way leading far beyond traditional logic. What distinguishes the new logic from the old logic is,[4] on the one hand, the use of symbols, in analogy to mathematics, in symbolic logic, and on the other hand the addition of entirely new domains to logic: besides predicates, the exclusive concern of traditional logic, relations and propositional functions, i.e., propositions with blanks filled by variables. The reconstruction of the content of logic originated from mathematicians who found traditional logic an unsatisfactory tool for the rigorous construction of mathematics. The propositions of mathematics cannot be fitted into the judgmental schema of traditional logic (subject-copula-predicate) since they assert relations. Propositions which ascribe a predicate to a subject are suitable only for properties, or classes; relations, consisting in the coordination of two or more terms, cannot be adequately expressed in this manner. And series, which are so important in mathematics, can be constructed only in terms of asymmetrical transitive relations. For this reason a logical theory of relations had to be developed. Furthermore, logical difficulties emerged in the theoretical construction of mathematics, in that antinomies arose, partly of a general logical character, and this was another reason for reforming logic. The reconstruction of logic was comprehensively and with finality achieved in Russell and Whitehead's great work "Principia mathematica", vol. I-III, 1910-13, second edition 1925-27. The new logic has been cultivated and furthered not only by students of Russell (Wittgenstein, Ramsey) but also by the Polish schools of symbolic logic in Warsaw, Lemberg and Krakow, by Hilbert and his students, by H. Scholz in Muenster and K. Duerr in Zürich, by Joergensen in Kopenhagen and Kaila in Helsinki, and in the United States.

The new logic, symbolic logic, is far superior to traditional logic, both in terms of content and in terms of form. It not only contains a larger number of essential disciplines, but even the old disciplines are treated with greater rigor and more systematically. And with the help of symbolism a form of representation has been found which enables mathematically precise formulation of concepts and propositions and rules governing the latter's combination. Thus it becomes possible to operate in a purely formal manner without regard to content, a sort of calculus of concepts and propositions. This leads to a degree of clarity and rigor which is unattainable within ordinary language. Equivocations are avoided, unnoticed assumptions are revealed, rigorous deduction is guaranteed. It must be admitted, though, that noticeable limits are imposed upon the use of symbolic logic by the circumstance that the formulae become soon too complicated. "It would, of course, be practically impossible to give each deduction which occurs the form of a complete derivation in the logical calculus, i.e., to dissolve it into single steps of such a kind that each step is the application of one of the rules of transformation of the calculus, including the definitions. An ordinary reasoning of a few seconds would then take days. But it is essential that this dissolution is theoretically possible and practically possible for any small part of the process. Any critical point can thus be put under the logical microscope". "If some persons want to come to an agreement about the formal correctness of a given derivation, they may leave aside all differences of opinion on material questions or questions of interpretation. They simply have to examine whether or not the given series of formulas fulfils the formal rules of the calculus."[5]

In "Principia mathematica" Russell and Whitehead deduced mathematics from the system of the new logic. The primitive concepts of mathematics are constructed out of the primitive concepts of logic alone, on the basis of the logical postulates with the addition of only two new postulates, the axioms of infinity and of choice. The natural numbers as well as the more complex types of number, the concepts of analysis and of set theory, are all constructed in this manner. Thus mathematics is reduced to a branch of logic, and what holds of logic therefore also holds of mathematics.

The new logic and its relationship to mathematics had decisive importance for the philosophical orientation of the Vienna Circle. The latter acquired in this way a proper sense for the distinctive character of logic and mathematics, a sense lacking among traditional empiricists. Traditional empiricism, as classically formulated by J. St. Mill and Spencer and as represented still at the present time,[6] believed that even mathematics and logic must be empirically validated. The latter were interpreted simply as the most extensive generalizations from experience, the most fundamental laws of being and of thought, entirely abstract and formalized. In that case these sciences would contain laws of nature, and then they would be inductive—and therefore refutable by experience.

This point of view is wholly untenable. After all, if discrepancies between mathematical propositions and observations occur, nobody would for a moment think of declaring the mathematical propositions as refuted and of revising them in the light of experience. Rather we regard the theorems as more certain than our counting and measurements. For if the latter lead to contradictions with the former, we reject our measurements as insufficiently precise and our counting as mistaken. This proves that mathematics is not based on experience, but is valid independently of experience. Nor is logic derivable from experience, since all controlled empirical inquiry presupposes logic. How could logic ever be changed by new experience! *Genetically,* indeed, logic and mathematics are reducible to experience, i.e. series of impressions, and the latter no doubt constitute the original occasion for their development; but the systems thus created are entirely self-sufficient, their validity in no way depends upon experience; they are valid "a priori", provided we understand by this term no more than "independent of experience". This cannot be denied.

This insight has so far stood as a decisive objection against empiricism and made the latter untenable in the eyes of anybody who has the insight. The way out of the dilemma "abandonment of empiricism or misinterpretation of logic and mathematics" was first shown by the Vienna Circle:[7] logic and mathematics make no assertions about empirical reality. Logic offers no knowledge, it does not formulate the fundamental laws of being but the foundations of conceptual order. Logical relations are merely conceptual relations, they are not factual relations within the empirical world, but only relations within the symbolic system. Classes, e.g., are nothing real but only conceptual syntheses. And you cannot find in your environment peculiar negative facts, along with positive facts, corresponding to the concept of negation. Since logical relations are purely formal, they can be ascertained <u>without any regard to the specific meanings of propositions, the concrete states of affairs</u>. Consequently they cannot assert anything about reality. What logic contains are principles of order among symbolic representations. Linguistically formulated thinking involves combination of symbols and the coordination of symbols to objects and their relations. These coordinations are not unique, such that one and only one symbol would correspond to each object and relation and conversely, but <u>many-one, i.e. several symbols or complexes of symbols</u> <u>correspond to the same object</u>, but not conversely. For this reason mutual transformations of complexes of symbols which all designate the same object or state of affairs are possible. It is the rules of such transformations that constitute the content of logic. Pure logic establishes only laws within the symbolic system, not laws of the empirical world. <u>The well-known logical principle</u> "what is true of all, is true of each" merely expresses the same fact by two different symbolizations, viz. by "all" and by "each". But "it is not a property of the *world*, that what is true of all is also true of each".[8]

Mathematics, being deducible from logic, shares the nature of logic. In mathematics likewise no factual assertions are made. In pure mathematics numbers do not signify, if we abstract from their application, empirical objects, and geometry is no description of real space. Indeed, there are several mutually incompatible geometries; which of these applies to the empirical world cannot be decided a priori. Thus they are cultivated for their own sake regardless of their applicability. Systems of pure geometry are not concerned with <u>empirical objects</u> but with <u>ideal entities, like the unextended point</u>, etc. An equation, like Kant's famous example $7+5=12$, does not designate a real state of affairs but expresses a transformation of two groups of units into a single group in accordance with the rules of arithmetic. These units are not empirical objects nor are the rules of arithmetic their empirical laws; numbers are syntheses of classes of thinkable elements of any sort, and the rules of arithmetic are the rules, stipulated by us, for the transformation of such classes into others.[9] All that happens in this process is that the *same* units are brought into different arrangements. The entire process occurs within the symbolic system, within a purely conceptual order.[10]

Thus interpreted, the a priori validity of logic and mathematics poses no difficult problems. Such validity can easily be accepted since it does not concern experience at all but only symbolic representation. The propositions of logic and mathematics cannot be interpreted as knowledge of reality but only as modes of symbolic transformation to which there always corresponds in the world one and the same state of affairs—indeed, this correspondence *must* hold. Their a priori validity derives from conventions which refer only to the domain of symbolisation and can therefore be laid down with a priori validity; for they do not determine laws of nature but only laws of symbolism.

The propositions of mathematics are not synthetic, as Kant and Mill had believed, but analytic; they can be known to be true (or false) solely on the basis of the definitions of the concepts; in terms of which they are constituted; they are merely tautologies, Wittgenstein's term for propositions recognizable as true already by their logical form. The analytic character of mathematics is clearly revealed by its construction in the form of deductive systems, a method of construction current since the latter half of the nineteenth century. Its analytic character explains its a priori validity. It deals only with conceptual connections, not with empirical reality. Therefore there is no need to look for a ground of validity of synthetic a priori judgments, and neither "pure reason" nor "pure intuition", neither "Intuition" nor "Evidenz" nor even experience is required to provide such a ground. Analytic relations are logical, not empirical, and logical relations are only relations within a symbolic system. The autonomy of logic results from the fact that logic contains, not the fundamental laws of the world, but the fundamental laws of thinking about the world. Thus the autonomy of logic and mathematics with respect to experience is easily justified.

Obviously, the discovery of the independent validity of logic and mathematics was not original with the Vienna Circle; this conception is very old. The insight into the analytic character of mathematics likewise had a precedent. It was expressed in detail by Couturat,[11] and even earlier Brentano defended this thesis.[12] But most of those earlier philosophers who had recognized the a priori nature of logic and mathematics were apriorists and rationalists even with regard to knowledge of reality. Empiricists, on the other hand, failed to see their a priori nature. Only the Vienna Circle knew how to combine insight into the latter with empiricism.[13] This constitutes a fundamental revision of empiricism, and the solution is immensely significant. The earlier claim of empiricism to derive all knowledge and science from experience as the sole ground of validity is thus abandoned. The empiricist thesis now restricts itself to factual knowledge. All synthetic judgments are to be validated by experience; there is no other way of establishing their validity.

This core of empiricism is preserved. However, recognition of the a priori validity of logic and mathematics does not entail rationalism with respect to factual knowledge, since neither of these sciences makes any factual assertions at all. In this way empiricism has been subjected to a thorough-going reform which provides it with a tenable foundation, hitherto lacking. In a sense the dualism of rationalism and empiricism remains: there are basically two classes of assertions, those which are necessary, valid independently of experience, and factual assertions, synthetic propositions, which are refutable and valid only on the basis of experience. The former are valid on logical grounds alone, they are all of them analytic propositions devoid of factual content. But this dualism is not absolute, as it used to be. Rational knowledge does not reveal a world beyond the empirical world; metaphysical rationalism has been abandoned. Logic itself admits of incorporation into experience, in that it can be pragmatically interpreted as a definite form of rational behavior.[14]

The described restriction of empiricism is reflected by the label attached to the Vienna Circle's point of view: "logical empiricism".[15] Indeed, this title has been advocated by its leading members, such as Schlick[16] and Carnap.[17] The latter objected to the names "logical positivism"[18] and "neo-positivism",[19] usually given to the movement, that they "suggest too close an affiliation with the older positivism, especially of Comte and Mach".[20] But one could raise a perfectly analogous objection against the name "empiricism". For here the difference from the older empiricism is no less significant. The Vienna Circle shares with traditional positivism, after all, the restriction

of all positive knowledge to the special sciences and of
philosophy to the logic of science.[21]

II. *Logical Analysis of Language*

The new logic has been developed as a tool for the
theoretical construction of mathematics; in the Vienna
Circle it becomes the tool for the logical analysis of
science in general. Applied logic, as contrasted with
pure logic, was used to make the procedure of philosophical inquiry more exact.[22] The requirement of scientific
philosophy left the Vienna Circle no choice with regard
to the method of inquiry. Its problem areas were primarily two: the analysis of knowledge and the theoretical
foundations of, first, mathematics, and secondly, the
natural sciences, but likewise of psychology and sociology.

Epistemology used to be, by and large, a confused
mixture of psychological and logical investigations, even
in quite a few of the earlier writings of the Vienna
Circle itself. Psychological investigations belong to the
domain of factual knowledge and must be conducted by
using the methods of empirical science. Thus they do
not belong in epistemology. The latter can be nothing
else but the logical analysis of knowledge, "logic of science", as it came to be called in the Vienna Circle in order
to make this point unmistakably clear.

The basic concepts and foundations of the special
sciences involve space and time, causality and determin-
ism, and so forth. The logic of science is not concerned
with an *empirical* analysis of these concepts, which is the
task of the special sciences, but only with *logical* analysis.
Whatever question is a question of fact must be answered
by some one of the special sciences, and is thus no philos-

25

ophical question. The latter kind of question can concern only the logical structure of scientific knowledge.

To inquire into the logical structure of scientific knowledge is to inquire into the logical connections of the concepts and propositions of science, into how some concepts involve others, how some propositions are deducible from others and the like. It is this kind of inquiry, the logical analysis of concepts, propositions, proofs, hypotheses, theories of science, which constitutes epistemology, indeed philosophy in general. This inquiry alone is distinctively philosophical, and the subject-matter, task and method of philosophy is thus determined. This problem area, however, extends beyond the problems of traditional epistemology. It contains such problems as:[23] do two concepts B_1 and B_2 whose definitions differ have the same meaning? Are two sentences which differ verbally synonymous? Is sentence S_2 a purely logical consequence of sentence S_1? Or does it follow only by virtue of a law of nature? Is theory T_1 compatible or incompatible with theory T_2? If compatible, is T_2 contained in T_1 or does it go beyond T_1? If the latter—by virtue of which components? Or, in terms of concrete illustrations: "Is the principle of the constancy of the velocity of light, in the theory of relativity, a convention or a factual proposition? Is the general theory of relativity logically inconsistent?" "What is the meaning of probability statements?" Since science, as we come down to its empirical basis, presupposes ordinary, everyday knowledge, the logic of science amounts to the logical analysis of knowledge in general.

Knowledge is formulated in linguistic expressions, and only the latter render its conceptual content fixed and objective; it is only linguistic expression which gives solid and permanent form to the ideas and enables their communication. Language, however, serves more than the purpose of communication, of intersubjective understanding, it is even solipsistically indispensable, as means of representation. Without language it would be utterly impossible to develop and master the manifold of concepts and propositions. Language constitutes, so to speak, the body of knowledge, the latter could not be built up without it. Consequently, the logical analysis of scientific knowledge must be applied to the latter's linguistic expression. While inquiry into *facts,* i.e., *that which* language represents, is the business of the special sciences, logical analysis is aimed at the form in which facts are linguistically formulated through concepts and propositions. Thus linguistic analysis constitutes the proper domain of the logic of science. The logical analysis of an expression consists in its inclusion in a definite linguistic system which must be determined by indicating the essential constituents of that expression.[24]

Of course, this kind of linguistic analysis must be distinguished from linguistics. What is analyzed is not a natural language actually in use, but a language in simplified and perfected form. It is linguistic structure in general, that which is indispensable for the expression of thoughts in any language whatsoever. In addition to its referential function, language also serves to express feelings and attitudes, but logical analysis is concerned only with the referential function. Language is not studied from a psychological nor from a sociological point of view but solely with reference to the general conditions of a system of symbolization. It is the latter which is here meant by "language".

Language in this sense is representation of a subject-

matter by a system of signs, especially by sounds and inscriptions but also by gestures, as in the language of deaf-
mutes, by flag signals and other signs. Signs have a meaning, this is what makes them signs rather than noises or
shapes. They refer beyond themselves, to conceptual and
propositional meanings which they represent. Therefore
the study of language does not involve oblivion to the
essential, the conceptual content. For it is in the structure
of language that the structure of thought shows itself,
and this is why by apprehending the former one appre-
hends the latter. This correspondence is the stricter the
greater the precision with which ideas are linguistically
formulated. The significance of symbolic logic for linguistic analysis lies just in the achievement of precision.
The use of symbolic logic is thus justified as something
more than mere "dressing".

Language as a system of signs can be looked at from
two points of view: one may concentrate on the representative function of language, on that which it represents, or one may concentrate on the form of representation. In the former case one is concerned with the significance of signs, their semantic function, in the latter
case with the manner of their combination, their syntactic rules. If one adopts the first point of view one will
also pay attention to the vocabulary of a language;
if one adopts the second point of view one is exclusively
interested in the grammar of a language. For there to be
language, both vocabulary and grammar are needed.[25]

It is, however, possible to abstract at times from the
semantic dimension of a language and focus attention,
in purely formal manner, upon the formation of signs
and sign-combinations. In that case material analysis is
replaced by formal analysis. The formal, structural pro-

28

perties, on which the representative function of language is based, are then studied by themselves.

In describing the structure of a language and stating its essential forms by means of definitions and rules, one talks about language itself. Whether this is indeed possible, and if so, how, has been the subject of considerable controversy in the Vienna Circle. Language itself then occupies the position which is usually occupied by the objects about which assertions are made. Consequently the need was felt to introduce, over and above the language referred to, a second language by means of which the first language can be referred to, a "meta-language". But in order to describe the structure of the meta-language a new language is needed and in order to talk about the latter still another and so forth ad inf. Wittgenstein, however, declared it as impossible to make assertions about language.[26] The formal structure of a language cannot be talked about, it only shows itself. That two sentences contradict each other, or one follows from the other, is shown by their logical structure. All we can do is to identify the common form of several sentences. But if it is impossible to make assertions about language, then all lingustic analysis consists of nothing but meaningless pseudo-sentences. As Wittgenstein says with regard to the statements in his own Tractatus,[27] they can be no more than practical instruments for the clarification of genuine statements but no theoretical assertions. We thus confront the paradoxical thesis that it is completely impossible to express a theory of language in meaningful sentences.

But all these difficulties have been solved by Carnap in his "Logical Syntax of Language". There he has shown that the structure of a language can be represented by means of that very language. The meta-language is then a sub-language of the language investigated (see later p. 63). Thus a firm basis is provided, for the first time, for the whole enterprise of linguistic analysis, and it becomes possible to characterize, in scientific manner, the pervasive logical structure of language.

1. *Semantic Analysis*

(a) *Meaning, Meaninglessness and Metaphysics.*

Clarification of language with respect to its semantic function was one of the first efforts of the Vienna Circle.[28] To specify the meaning of a sign is to stipulate a relation of symbolization between a sign, i.e., a class of objects, and something signified, i.e., some object or class of objects (in the broadest sense), such that the sign refers to the signified and represents it. This requires knowledge of both the sign and the signified, each must be capable of being indicated. Hence it is impossible to stipulate a meaning whose object cannot be identified in some way or other. The meaning of a *word* can be specified by *definition*, i.e., by describing it in terms of other words whose meaning is already given, such that the former word can be replaced by the latter. But since this procedure cannot be continued indefinitely, we must eventually reach undefinable words, primitive concepts. Their meanings can be indicated only by the method used in learning the practical use of a language: by *pointing at* that which is designated by the word, the object falling under the concept. This is not always as simple a matter as it is with such words as "blue" or "hot". If we wish to make the meanings of words like "chance", "because", "immediately" intelligible we have to present complex situations in which these words are used. Thus Einstein fixed the meaning of "distant simultaneity" by describing an experimental method for determining distant simultaneity. Thus he indicated the conditions under which this word is to be used; he laid down the "grammar" of this word, as Wittgenstein, from whom this approach originates, put it.

When the locution "the way it is used" is applied to a *proposition,* it means "the state of affairs designated by it", which is equivalent to the conditions under which it is accepted as true or false. The meaning of a proposition is determined by its method of verification.[29] But what is relevant here is not *actual* verification of a statement but only possible verification, verifiability in principle. Actual verification is necessary for determining the truth of a proposition but not for determining its meaning. After all, a proposition could not become meaningful only after its verification. For in order to carry out the procedure of verification one must know beforehand under what circumstances the proposition would be true.

Also, with regard to the *possibility* of verification, we must still distinguish between empirical and logical verifiability. Verification is *empirically* possible if its conditions do not contradict the laws of nature. Verification is *logically* possible if the structure of the proposition does not contradict the rules of logic, if it does not contradict the rules of application of the constituent terms. The meaningfulness of a statement depends only on the logical possibility, not the empirical possibility, of verifying it. We cannot verify the assertion "there is a mountain, three thousand feet high, on the other side of the moon", nevertheless it is not without meaning. This is because

31

its verification is made impossible only by contingent, empirical circumstances, not by logical principles. Thus even the assertions of Newtonian physics about absolute motion are not meaningless, since it is, within the framework of Newtonian physics, possible to state criteria for the truth or falsehood of these assertions. Michelson's experiment constituted not only a conceptual but even a practical possibility of verification. On the other hand, a sentence like "there is a world in itself, but it is wholly unknowable" is devoid of real content; it only seems to be meaningful because the constituent terms "there is", "world", "knowable" are meaningful. But in denying the knowability of this world we make it in principle impossible to find out whether there is such a world. And thus verification is ruled out on logical grounds. For it is impossible to describe what it would be like for this sentence to prove true. Such a sentence evokes, indeed, pictures, possibly even feelings, but this is not to say that it asserts a fact, or has theoretical content. It is internally inconsistent in that it claims knowledge of the existence of a world which is characterized as unknowable (It is not true that we must presuppose the meaningfulness of a self-contradictory statement in order to be able to tell that it is self-contradictory. The contradiction is apparent from the syntactic form of the sentence alone).

The above distinction between meaningfulness and meaninglessness applies to the theoretical, i.e., representative content of assertions. Hence "meaningless" means only: devoid of such content, empty as regards theoretical sense, but not: nonsensical.

Definitions are ultimately reducible to ostentation of what is designated. One can point only at something which is immediately given, and thus only at what is perceivable. In this way, what assertions can possibly mean is tied to experience, there can be no super-empirical meaning. No meaning can be given to that which is not reducible to experience; and this is a consequence of fundamental importance. For we have thus found a clear criterion for delimiting scientific knowledge from metaphysics,[30] an objective the Vienna Circle has been devoted to from the very start. "Metaphysics" means a claim to knowledge such as is inaccessible to empirical science, knowledge which transcends the latter. For metaphysical sentences it is altogether impossible to specify a method of verification, they are not reducible to what may be empirically given, and therefore they are without specifiable meaning. They are merely combinations of words which look like meaningful sentences; they are mere pseudo-statements.

Such sentences may arise in two ways: by containing a word which has no meaning, which represents only a pseudo-concept, or by a juxtaposition of meaningful words in a manner which contradicts the rules of logical grammar. A word represents a pseudo-concept if the conditions of meaning-specification have not been met for it, i.e., according to what was said above, if no empirical criteria for application of the concept can be stated. Such words are, e.g., "Urgrund", "the unconditioned, absolute", "being in itself", "nichten". A pseudo-concept may also arise, for example, if a word like "nothing" is used like a thing-name, while legitimately it can serve only for the formulation of a negative existential statement. This leads to pseudo-statements because one wishes to make assertions about this supposed object "nothing".

Pseudo-statements are sentences which do not violate

the grammatical rules in the philological sense and therefore look like genuine statements, e.g., "Caesar is a prime
number", which is like "Caesar is a field commander".
This shows that traditional, philological grammar is unsatisfactory. The customary classification of kinds of
words into substantives, adjectives, verbs, etc. needs to be
supplemented by further subdivisions of these classes
into syntactic categories in accordance with the classes of
entities designated by the words of those kinds: things
or thing-properties or thing-relations, numbers or num-
ber-properties or number-relations etc. Number-proper-
ties cannot be predicated of things, by virtue of their
very definitions. For this reason the sentence "Caesar is
a prime number" could not even be formulated in a
logically perfect language. In such a language metaphysical sentences of this kind could not be formulated either.

Thus the pseudo-statements of metaphysics cannot
serve the function of representation of facts at all; their
function is quite different: they express an attitude
towards life, what they manifest are affective and volitional attitudes towards the environment and society and
the tasks of life. This is why metaphysics is of such value
to so many. Life-feelings may also find expression through
artistic creation. To this extent metaphysics is analogous
to works of art. The difference is that metaphysics is the
expression of such feeling through a system of sentences
which seem to stand in logical relations, relations of deducibility to one another, and thus arises the illusion of
theoretical content.

The meaning of a sentence consists in the latter's
verifiable content. Only assertions about empirical facts
admit of verification. Hence sentences about what is in
principle beyond experience have no meaning. It is thus

that scientific and metaphysical sentences are sharply distinguished as meaningful and meaningless. But thereby a thesis of traditional empiricism is again surrendered, according to which, as Hume supposed, the impossibility of metaphysics is due to the insolubility of its problems. But there are no insoluble problems in the sense that an answer is *in principle* impossible.[31] It may indeed happen that a question is *practically* incapable of being answered, on account of technical difficulties, like the question about the geography of the other side of the moon, or on account of a lack of relevant factual knowledge, like the question "What was Plato doing on his fiftieth anniversary?" For these reasons questions may be just at the time unanswerable, or even presumably for all time. But this does not mean that they preclude an answer in principle, as a logical impossibility. For one can readily think of the conditions under which a given answer to such a question would be true. But if this cannot be done, then the question itself is without meaning. Since the meaningfulness of a sentence is determined by its verifiability in principle, questions are indirectly, by reference to their answers, divided into meaningful and meaningless ones. There cannot be questions that are in principle unanswerable since such questions cannot even be meaningfully asked. Those questions which have made their appearance in philosophy from the very beginning of philosophy can either be rendered meaningful by careful formulation, or else they cannot, in which case they cannot even be meaningfully asked.

But the verifiability criterion of meaning has still another consequence. It follows that only empirical statements are meaningful, for they alone are verifiable. Mathematical and logical statements, on the other hand, are devoid of meaning. The Vienna Circle did draw this consequence. The claim is easily understood if one keeps in mind that meaning is identified with representative content. For mathematical and logical statements are no assertions about facts, they do not express knowledge of this kind, they are only rules. Mathematical statements are rules for the employment of symbols—looked at in this way, mathematics is a pure calculus—, logical statements are rules for the transformation of sentences into others.[32] But even then the statements of the logic of science are devoid of content, since they are logical. Wittgenstein already drew this radical consequence of the verifiability theory of meaning. "My statements elucidate by virtue of the fact that he who understands them recognizes them in the end as meaningless, if he has by means of them—upon them—climbed beyond them."[33] The propositions of the logic of science are only precepts which are supposed to direct one's eye upon what shows itself through language. As such they lack theoretical content.

But the adoption of this verifiability criterion of meaning was soon subjected to incisive criticism. First Petzaell pointed out some untenable consequences of this conception of meaning,[34] and then Ingarden emphasized that the latter implies that "metalogical" sentences are non-sensical;[35] also Weinberg made the same point.[36] Lewis objected against the "postulate of empirical significance" that it narrowed the circle of philosophical discussion intolerably.[37] Likewise Nagel,[38] Stace[39] and Reichenbach[40] raised objections. In the Vienna Circle, Neurath first stood up against meaningless comments. Popper, in his *Logik der Forschung,* a book which contained several important suggestions, held against the entire theory of meaning that it amounted to an arbitrary stipulation. "Nothing is easier than to expose a question as a meaningless pseudo-problem: all one needs to do is to define the concept of 'significance' narrowly enough so that any inconvenient question may be disposed of by the declaration that it is impossible to find any sense in it; and after having recognized the questions of empirical science as the only 'meaningful' ones, even debates concerning the concept of meaning become meaningless: once this meaning-dogma has been elevated on the throne, it is forever beyond assault, 'untouchable and final' ",[41] as Wittgenstein puts it in the preface to his book. Later Carnap subjected this criterion of meaning to a thoroughgoing critique and revision, in his essay "Testability and Meaning"[42] which is in many ways of fundamental importance. He admits that the definition of meaningfulness in terms of verifiability is too narrow. For it implies the meaninglessness of sentences which can hardly be denied to be meaningful. Thus the denial of an analytic sentence (e.g., the Kantian example: "all bodies are extended") would result in a meaningless sentence, since it produces a self-contradictory sentence, and so one which is in principle unverifiable. Conversely, by denying a meaningless self-contradictory sentence (e.g., "the total height of the tower of the Vienna City Hall is both 50 m and 100 m"), we would obtain a meaningful, because verifiable, sentence. Two synthetic sentences, individually meaningful but mutually incompatible (e.g., "the tower of the Vienna City Hall has a height of 50 m" and "the tower of the Vienna City Hall has a height of 100 m"), would, if combined into a conjunction, produce a meaningless sentence since their conjunction is an unverifiable contradiction. All this shows that the definition of meaningfulness in terms of verifiability amounts to no sufficient criterion of distinction between meaningful and meaningless sentences.

In order to gain clarity about the concept of meaning one has to enter into a thorough analysis of language with respect to its semantic function. A semantic, representative system consists of signs, as its elements, and their combinations. The signs may be words or flags or drum beats, any kind of elements whatever. There are semantic systems, languages, which consist only of signs and combinations with fixed, rigid meanings, e.g., flag- or drumlanguages. Likewise animal languages contain only signals for definite kinds of events. In such languages only situations for which definite sign-complexes have been agreed upon admit of symbolization. What distinguishes human language from animal language is just that through combinations of signs ever new meanings, without prior stipulation for the individual case, can be expressed; that is, by means of a limited number of signs it can represent an unlimited number of situations, simply by combining the signs in ever new ways. What makes this possible is the circumstance that the meaning of a given combination of signs is not determined by a special convention, but by general rules of combination. These rules are laid down in the grammar of a language.

In such a language signs are, according to their meanings, divided into two classes:[43] descriptive signs, designating things, properties, relations, and formative or logical signs, which serve to combine descriptive signs into sentences and to characterize their truth-conditions. The descriptive signs are either names (of things) or designations of properties or relations, one-place or many-place predicates. The logical signs are either constants like "not", "and", "or", "if-then", "is", "all", or variables which designate blanks to be filled with names or predicates or sentences.

The semantic formation-rules determine the manner in which out of such signs sequences of signs designating situations, that is propositions, may be constructed. They permit the concatenation of a name (in the case of a relation, of several names) with a predicate, further negations, conjunctions, disjunctions, implications, existential and universal sentences. The concatenation of a name with a predicate constitutes the simplest form of sentence; the other forms are sentences containing sentences as components. The formation-rules also include those which result from the logical theory of types with regard to the combinatory possibilities of classes of descriptive signs. The meanings of logical constants can be fixed by semantic rules, by indicating generally what a sentence formed by means of a given logical constant designates. For example, the joining of a name S to a predicate P by "is" signifies that the object designated by S has the property or relation designated by P.[44] Or: "not"—P signifies any proposition other than the proposition designated by "P".

Thus the conditions are stated which determine the meaning of a sign-combination constituting a sentence. By fixing the meaning of the descriptive as well as the logical signs, and regulating, by means of the formation rules, their combination into sentences, one determines completely the meaning of a sign-combination, i.e., a sentence. It consists in whatever is designated by the combination according to the given meanings of the signs and the given formation rules. In other words: meaning is simply determined by the vocabulary and the—logical! —grammar of a language.[45]

But thus it is clear that whether or not a sentence is meaningful depends on the stipulated semantic and syntactic rules for a given language. A sign is meaningless only if nothing has been coordinated to it by a stipulation; and a sign-combination is a pseudo-statement if no coordination to it of some state of affairs results from the stipulated semantic and syntactic rules. Since different rules may be stipulated for the same signs, a sentence which is meaningless in one language may be meaningful in a language of different construction. A sentence like "the sky is laughing" could, if taken literally, be regarded as just as meaningless as the sentence "the stone is sad", if the syntactic rules forbid the application of psychological predicates to the class of inorganic entities. But if this is not the case, then it is a meaningful sentence which is merely false. And if "laughing" here designates, by a shift of meaning, not a mental state but the power to evoke a mental state (making one feel gay), then the sentence becomes meaningful and true. Whether a sentence is meaningful or meaningless, cannot be decided in straightforward manner by considering the sentence in isolation. For this depends upon the structure of the language. Meaning is not absolute, but is always determined in relation to a semantic and syntactic system.

Here again we have a significant insight. For thus the distinction, at first sight so obvious, between scientific knowledge and metaphysics collapses. We cannot any more dispose of metaphysical sentences by simply calling them meaningless. On the contrary, it must be conceded that one could even construct a semantic system in which metaphysical sentences are meaningful—a point which was always stressed by the Polish logisticians. But all that follows is that we must cease representing the distinction between metaphysics and science as one dictated by language *in general*. For there exists more than one single language, there is a plurality of possible languages accordingly as we choose this or that set of semantic and syntactic rules. Now, the fundamental postulates of empiricism select from all these languages a definite one: a language satisfying the requirements of (1) reducibility of the meanings of the descriptive signs to ostentation of that which signs designate, indeed, of what is given in experience, (2) empirical testability of factual assertions, which again means ultimately possibility of pointing to experiential data. By the stipulation of these conditions the meaning of words and assertions is restricted to possible experience, tied to what is given in experience. In a language of this character the sentences of transcendental metaphysics remain meaningless and unverifiable and are thus clearly distinguished from scientific assertions. The criterion of distinction does not, indeed, result from the conditions of language in general, of each and every possible language, but with respect to the special language of empiricism it remains valid.

(b) *Content and Structure*

If we wish to understand the semantic function of language, it is essential that we be clear about what is capable of being designated and communicated by language. This problem also has been thoroughly dealt with by the Vienna Circle. The elements of a sentence, words, designate in the ultimate analysis nothing but what can be pointed to, data of experience, that is. Such data are

41

qualitative, like sensory qualities, qualities of feelings or other psychical qualities. But this qualitative content does not admit of linguistic communication. You cannot communicate qualitative content to somebody by means of words and sentences. It is a truism that one cannot explain to a blind person what color is, nor what home-sickness is to somebody who has never been away from home. We describe qualitative content, e.g. a given color shade, by specifying the relations of this content to others. We say, e.g., it is the color possessed by such and such a kind of object (brick-red, or pigeon-gray), or the color resembling a definite color in a color-chart, or the color which is somewhat brighter or darker or more saturated than some other color. Thus a qualitative content is described in terms of its position in a manifold, by placing it within the manifold: it is described "structurally", in other words. It can be determined only through its relationships, only implicitly; the qualitative content as such is not uniquely definable. What is inter-subjectively transmitted through linguistic designations ("blue", "sweet") is not the qualitative content itself, but its position within some intersubjective order.

Consequently it is not possible either to determine whether two people perceiving the same object, e.g. a sample of green against a red background, experience the same qualitative content. Whoever investigates this matter with all available means of experimental psychology, will never discover more than that the subjects react in the same (or different) manner, that they make concordant (or divergent) assertions; that is, all he can verify is that the qualities experienced by each of the subjects stand in identical (or different) relations to other qualities. If the investigation shows that one subject has normal vision and the other is red-green-blind, one still does not know the nature of the qualities themselves but merely that they stand in different relationships. Qualitative content as such cannot be controlled, it belongs to the private sphere of each person and is inaccessible to anyone else.[46]

Thus the qualitative is not communicable but can only be experienced. And experience is always my experience (unless telepathic co-experience occurs). All that is communicable is the position of the qualitative within some order. Designations of the qualitative have a sharable content only to the extent that they refer to such positions; this alone makes them intersubjective. "Color" designates intersubjectively something dependent on the functioning of eyes, "sound" something dependent on the functioning of ears, "feeling" something with definite expressive symptoms. This also holds for psychology, not only for experimental psychology but likewise for introspective psychology. The latter's assertions too can have no other content but ordinal relations, "structure".

It is not just the propositions of science, but also all other intersubjective propositions, including those of poetry, which cannot communicate anything else but structure. For poetry, indeed, intuition and feeling, and thus qualitative content, is essential, but poetry does not communicate the latter, it only evokes them. That which is communicated through poetry gives rise all by itself to images and feelings in the reader or hearer. Such is also the procedure of historical description, if the purpose is not just to describe and causally explain the actions of protagonists and the spiritual climate of an epoch, but to produce an understanding of the latter. The intention of the historian is in that case to produce a re-living of the events, a qualitative experience, by means of historical information.

But we must never lose sight of the fact that what is here involved is the communicative function of language. This restriction by no means applies generally to its designative function.[47] Designation "is a kind of correspondence between two things" such that one stands for the other,[48] better a correspondence between two classes of phenomena, a class of sounds or inscriptions, which is what a word is, and a class of objects (in the widest sense), which is what is coordinated to the word. This coordination is ultimately established by pointing to data of experience. In doing this we supplement the word-language by gestures through which we refer to data of experience, and thus to qualitative contents and their relations. Insofar as the designation is used intersubjectively for purposes of communication, its meaning is determined only through relationships. The terms of these relations can be represented only by variables (just as in Hilbert's "Grundlagen der Geometrie" the geometric elements are determined as terms of the axiomatic relations). But what occurs in the process of understanding the designation is that each one of us substitutes for these variables qualitative contents from his own experience which are determined by these relationships. The designation is thus connected for each person individually with a subjective qualitative content, not just with a structure. The designation, then, has an individual-subjective meaning over and above its intersubjective meaning; for each individual it also designates a qualitative content known to him from his own experience. And each individual interprets the quality-designations contained in a given communication as referring to the qualities he has ex-

Erroneous view ↓

perienced himself. Everybody has his own interpretation for them. This kind of understanding consists in interpreting the designations in terms of the qualitative content corresponding to the communicated structure. Different people communicate to each other what is determined by these structural forms and it is the latter which they share and with respect to which they agree. The reason is that they all live in a common world—or putting it the other way around: this is the reason why they live in one and the same world. Each one of them, N however, fills this form with his own personal qualitative experiences, and thus establishes contact with his own world of experience. Whether they also agree in their qualitative *interpretation*, cannot be found out. For the qualitative is private and does not admit of comparison. The coordination of the designations with personally experienced qualities is indispensable and fundamental. The various intersubjective communications form only A a structural system, which acquires significance and utility for each individual only through application to his own experience. Each individual must be capable of establishing contact between the common intersubjective world and his own private, subjective world. It is only thus that the terms of the relations which constitute intersubjective meaning are secured a uniquely determined interpretation. For otherwise they are mere variables. Subjective, qualitative content thus forms the basis of everything that is intersubjective and objective, and is therefore indispensable.[49]

However, as Waismann reports in the foreword to Schlick's collected essays (p. XXVII, XXVIII), Schlick tried to get beyond the doctrine, developed in detail and with special emphasis, of the incommunicability of the qualitative. "The later writings—'Ueber die Beziehung zwischen psychologischen and physikalischen Begriffen' and 'Meaning and Verification'—show how Schlick abandoned in his own thinking this distinction between content and structure. He depicts in them—again under the influence of Wittgenstein—peculiar logically possible worlds in which the 'contents' of other minds would be accessible to us. And herewith the distinction between 'communicable' and 'incommunicable' has lost its original meaning".

In his essay "Form and Content" Schlick had declared it as a *logical* impossibility for a man to share another man's experiences, and held consequently that it was in principle impossible to find out whether the qualitative contents when two people perceive the same object are identical or different. But now he considered such a discovery as only empirically impossible. It is just a matter of fact that another person's experiences cannot be shared, but this is no logical impossibility. In order to show this —in the context of another consideration, viz. the refutation of solipsism, not with reference to the communicability of the qualitative—he analyzes the proposition "I can feel only *my* pain" with regard to its meaning. According to his analysis, what characterizes an experience as "mine" is its connection with a definite body, "my" body. In this way the proposition reads more precisely: "I can feel pain only when something happens to my body". But we can think of another possibility, a logical possibility since it is describable: I might feel pain even when something happens to the body of *another* person. Schlick considers this as equivalent to the proposition "I can feel someone else's pain". Thus the comparison of qualitative contents owned by different persons appears to be at least logically possible, though empirically impossible.

But the above speculative reasoning has not yet established this point. If "I" and the characterization of an experience as "mine" is defined by reference to a definite body, then the other person's pain is that pain which depends on the other person's body. Now, in order for *myself* to feel the other person's pain, this feeling of pain must also depend on *my* body, otherwise it is only the other person's pain and not a pain I feel. Consequently the other person's pain which is felt by me depends upon processes in *two* bodies, while the other person's pain depends solely on his body. Schlick, now, makes the tacit assumption that the other person's pain which *I* feel is precisely identical with the pain felt by the *other* person. But this assumption is arbitrary and need not be valid. For in this case the other person's pain stands in a twofold relationship: to *one* body and to *two* bodies, and it would be more plausible to assume that this difference in causal dependence involves a change of the pain's quality. Hence it still remains uncertain whether the qualitative contents of different people are or are not comparable.

2. *Syntactic Analysis*

(a) *Syntax and Logic*

The other aspect of language, contrasted with its semantic function, is its formal structure, the structure of the representative system. In this field Carnap has laid the foundations. In his *The Logical Syntax of Language,* 1934 [50], we have the first instance of a systematic treatment of the subject. But he does not confine himself to the essential structure of language, he is equally interested in the relation of language to logic. Wittgenstein was the first one to call attention to the relationship between language and logic.[51] The rules of logic turn out to be rules of language, being at the same time basic rules for the construction of a symbolic system. The structure of a language and its relationship to logic emerge with particular clarity if we study both language and logic as formalized systems. Just as logic has been treated in terms of general forms, abstracted from specific meanings, from the medieval symbolization of quantity and quality of judgments and of subject-, predicate- and middle-terms of arguments to the system of "Principia mathematica", so language likewise can be formalized by considering, in abstraction from its meaning, its general form exclusively. A formal analysis of language, i.e., of a representative system, has been undertaken by Hilbert in his "meta-mathematics" and by the Polish logisticians (Ajdukiewicz, Tarski, Lukasiewicz, Lesniewski) in their "meta-logic". Carnap has received suggestions from them, through Tarski.

From the formal point of view, symbols are looked at as mere patterns, visual or auditory, and sentences, which are concatenations of symbols, as mere symbol-sequences, formulae, and the deduction of sentences from others is interpreted as a transformation of certain symbol-sequences into others. Language is treated as a pure calculus. From this point of view, it appears like a game with figures according to fixed rules of the game. The significance and value of such a formalization lies, as usual, in the fact that the relevant is isolated from the irrelevant, and can, thus isolated, be grasped clearly and formulated with precision. It is the specific meanings of sentences which are in this context irrelevant; what matters is only relations of the most general kind. Carnap calls the structure of a representative system "syntax", even though "syntax" in the philological sense contains only the rules of combination of symbols. While it is the kinds of symbols which correspond in the formalized system to etymology, "grammar" is properly speaking the analogous term for the structure of representative systems. But since in a formalized system of language the rules for the combination of symbols, the syntactic rules, are particularly important, what matters above all are the rules of formation and transformation, in short "syntax".

It is not the syntax of an empirical, existing language, "descriptive" syntax, which is here referred to, but "pure" syntax, i.e. the "structure of possible serial order of arbitrary elements".[52] If one wishes to clarify the latter, one must not take the analysis of the syntax of some spoken language as a starting point, for this would be far too complicated. For this reason Carnap constructs to begin with two highly simplified model languages, in order to clarify syntactical structure in terms of them. In these languages objects are not designated by words but by numerals, just the way houses are designated by numerals instead of by proper names (as it used to be once upon a time), or the way spatial positions are designated by coordinates.[53] Properties and relations, the predicates attributed to these objects, admit likewise of designation by numerals to which signs referring to the *kinds* of properties or relations, "functors" so-called, are prefixed (e.g. "te (3) $= 5$" means: the temperature at position 3 equals 5, or "te diff $(3,4) = 2$" means: the temperature difference between positions 3 and 4 is 2). Functors are divided into descriptive ones, like those just adduced, and logico-mathematical ones, like e.g. "sum (3,4)", (that is, 3+4).

The first of the two formalized languages contains 11 elementary signs, above all the fundamental logical signs, then number-variables (x,y . . .) and number-constants (0, 1, 2 . . .), further predicates (represented by capital letters or groups of letters beginning with a capital) and functors (represented by groups of small letters). An ordered (finite) sequence of such signs, an "expression", is determined by the nature of the signs and their arrangement, by their syntactic forms. That which appears in ordinary language as a universal or existential sentence, is designated by the operators customary in symbolic logic. In the first one of the two languages only *restricted* operators occur, i.e. universal and existential operators which refer only to restricted domains of positions, not to all positions whatever. On the other hand, unrestricted universality applying, not to positions, but to symbols, is expressible by variables. E.g., "sum (x, y) = sum (y, x)" means: for any two numbers, the sum of the first and the second is equal to the sum of the second and the first. Finally, a characterization-operator is introduced, which serves in both languages specifically for the unique characterization of numbers and numerical relations. All these stipulations of symbols and formation-rules determine the elements and formal structure of this language.

But one further requires transformation-rules which determine under what conditions a sentence is derivable from others. The transformation-rules consist of axioms (strictly speaking, axiom-schemata, since the variables,

*And embody an implicit metaphysics as to what
Things, properties, relations & categories are the minimal necessary.
what are the reasons for the choices made?

required for axioms, representing "sentence", "predicate" and "functor", are not available in this language) and rules of derivation. The axioms amount to rules, in logistic notation, for the sentential calculus, the operators, the identity sign and the fundamental properties of the number-series. The rules of derivation define the concept "directly derivable" which is somewhat narrower than the concept "consequence"—a distinction clearly made only by modern logic.[54] The advantage and purpose of the simplified model language is that it facilitates considerably the definition of direct derivability and of the consequence-relation. A sentence is directly derivable if it results from another by substitution (in this case substitution of a numerical constant for a numerical variable) or if it is obtained by replacing a component of a sentence with a compound sentence (e.g. replacing an implication with "not . . . or . . .") or if it is implied by another sentence, or it may be directly derivable (considering that we are here dealing with numerical expressions) on the basis of the principle of mathematical induction.

Direct derivation is the basic procedure for any other kind of derivation. This procedure consists in a finite sequence of sentences such that each sentence is either a premise or a definition or directly derivable from a preceding sentence. On the basis of the definition of "derivable" the fundamental logico-syntactic concepts "provable", "refutable", "undecidable" can be defined. These concepts refer in the language under discussion only to finite sets of premises. For this reason they are narrower than the usual logical concepts "consequence", "analytic", "contradictory".[55] For the latter are applicable to *classes* of sentences which cannot be exhausted by a finite sequence. Sentential classes are syntactic forms of expressions. While a derivation is necessarily a finite sequence of sentences, a consequence can consist in a finite sequence of infinite classes of sentences. In terms of the concept of derivability and with the help of sentential classes it is also possible to define the concept of consequence,[56] which was undertaken by Carnap, with rigorous formulation, for the first time. On the basis of the definition of consequence it is then possible to define the important concepts "analytic", "synthetic", "contradictory", "consistent", "inconsistent". It is an original insight of the twentieth century—first formulated by Weyl,[57] then emphasized by Wittgenstein[58]—, that whether a sentence is analytic or contradictory can be decided independently of its meaning, on the basis of its logical structure alone. It is therefore possible to recognize the truth or falsehood of all logically decidable sentences from their symbolic form, provided the syntactic rules of the given language have been stated. By means of the concept of consequence it is also possible to determine the logical content of a sentence in purely formal manner, without any attention to its meaning being necessary. The logical content consists in the class of non-analytic sentences which are the consequences of the sentence in question. Thus what, according to the material interpretation, is known as the *meaning* of a sentence, is characterized in *formal manner*. In this way meaning-relationships are likewise describable in the formal idiom (e.g. synonymy).

The symbolic system thus constructed is by Carnap described as a "definite" language, because it uses only *restricted* universal and existential operators. (It may be compared perhaps to arithmetic of integers as interpreted finitistically by the mathematical intuitionists.)

The second symbolic system constructed by Carnap is an "indefinite" language. It contains the same symbols as the first, with only a single addition, but furthermore *unrestricted* operators. It is richer for other reasons too, since it contains the new kinds of functors and predicates and variables. Consequently the expressions must be segregated in accordance with their logical types and divided into levels. The various kinds of expressions of this language are, in analogy to those of the first language, specified by formation-rules. The transformation-rules likewise are for the most part analogous to those of the first language; additional axioms are demanded only by the greater wealth of symbols and by the unrestricted operators, except for the generalized axioms of choice by Zermelo and two axioms of extensionality. There are two rules of deduction, the rule of implication and the rule of the universal operator, which determine the conditions under which a sentence is directly deducible from others: if it is an implicate of another and if it is formed out of a given sentence by application of the universal operator. The definition of the concept of consequence is much more complicated in this language, owing to its superior richness as compared with the first language, and for this reason Carnap indicates only the method of definition, not the definition itself. Here, on the contrary, the concepts "analytic" and "contradictory" are defined first, and it is in terms of them that "consequence", "synthetic", "compatible", "incompatible" are subsequently defined. Once this is done, it can be proved that every logical sentence is either analytic or contradictory. With the help of a language of this kind the whole of classical mathematics and physics can be expressed.

On the basis of such preparatory work, the proper task can be solved: to construct a general syntax for any language whatever. For there is no such thing as *the* language, which Wittgenstein used to talk about, but there are several possible languages, as has just been shown in terms of the two languages constructed. By "general syntax" is meant a system of definitions of syntactic concepts which are applicable to all languages. As Carnap himself remarks (IV, p. 120), his system is only a sketch, a first attempt, with hardly any precedents to build upon.[59]

Indefinite concepts are indispensable for the construction of syntax. A linguistic sign is "indefinite" if there occurs an unrestricted operator in its definition-chain. The main concepts of transformation, viz. "derivable", "provable", "analytic", "contradictory", "synthetic", are definite only in greatly simplified systems, but usually indefinite. The concepts "consequence" and "logical content" are always indefinite. But whether indefinite concepts are legitimate is a matter of controversy. Whether a property expressed by a *definite* logical predicate of the first level is predicable in a given case, is always a decidable question. But for *indefinite* predicates there is no general decision procedure. For this reason indefinite concepts have been declared as meaningless and illegitimate by Poincaré, Brouwer and Wittgenstein. In contrast to this view, Carnap has shown that such concepts are meaningful and legitimate.

What led to the rejection of indefinite concepts as meaningless was the definition of "meaning" according to which the meaning of a concept is determined by the method for deciding whether the concept is predicable. A decision procedure of this kind for indefinite concepts is in general unknown, and therefore these concepts were regarded as meaningless. However, we know very well under what conditions a decision concerning the presence of a property expressed by an indefinite concept could be made. This is the case if we find a *proof* for the presence or absence of the property. Whether a sequence of sentences represents such a proof is definitely decidable. Thus indefinite concepts make sense, since we know under what conditions they apply. Even if one should lay down the narrow requirement that it should be decidable in each individual case whether the property expressed by an indefinite concept is present or not, one could not deny the legitimacy of these concepts. In order to establish the validity of a sentence containing an unrestricted operator, a general sentence, it is not necessary to prove each and every sentence derivable from it by substitution of constants; indeed, on account of the infinite number of such derivable sentences, this would be impossible. If such a procedure were necessary, all general sentences would indeed be undecidable and meaningless. But the general sentence can be established as valid by the construction of a single proof, which is a finite operation and consequently renders even sentences containing unrestricted operators provable. Thus "there is even for indefinite concepts . . . the possibility of arriving at a decision concerning their predicability in a given case, although we know of no procedure which guarantees such a decision in all cases" (p. 116, 117). Thus it is not necessary to exclude indefinite concepts.

The most important concept of general syntax is the concept of consequence. Once we determine its usage,

all logical relations within the given language are fixed
and definable. The definition of "direct consequence"
consists in conventions concerning the signs of the language, in formation- and transformation-rules. The rules
which implicitly define "consequence" are again distinguished from the rules which implicitly define "derivation", the latter involving the requirement that the properties of a derived sentence as well as of a class of sentences from which derivations are made be definite. The
syntactic concepts are divided into concepts of consequence and concepts of derivation according as reference is made in their definition to rules of consequence
or only to rules of derivation. A number of fundamental
concepts of consequence—valid and contravalid, determinate (either valid or contravalid) and indeterminate,
compatible and incompatible, logically dependent and
logically independent, complete and incomplete, content
and relations of content—are defined formally.

It should be noted that Carnap considers transformation-rules from an entirely general point of view. It
is customary to lay down in symbolic languages only such
transformation-rules as admit of logico-mathematical
validation; Carnap, however, admits also extra-logical
transformation-rules; laws of nature, or, generally speaking, empirical propositions, may be included in the
axioms. Accordingly a distinction is made between languages containing exclusively logico-mathematical transformation-rules and languages containing moreover
"physical" (in the broadest sense, i.e. empirical) transformation-rules ("L"-languages and "P"-languages). The
syntactic concepts, which in the most general conception
of "language" are set up in connection with both kinds of
transformation-rules—valid or contravalid, determinate

etc.—are more general than the concepts "analytic", "contradictory", "synthetic". "Analytic", "synthetic", etc. are concepts of a language-system containing only logical transformation-rules. If among the axioms there are axioms of empirical origin, then even the validity of a synthetic statement is by means of them provable, and the latter may consequently, just like an analytic statement, be knowable as true or false on the basis of its symbolic form alone. Carnap defined the distinction between logical and "physical" transformation-rules, a distinction based on the meaning of sentences, likewise in purely formal manner.

With regard to the matter of extra-logical transformation-rules, Schlick rightly objected, however, to the habit of speaking of the "adoption" of natural laws as axioms. In declaring a sentence which, presupposing ordinary grammar, expresses a natural law, as a syntactic rule, one implicitly assigns to such a sequence of symbols "an entirely new meaning, or rather, one deprives it of meaning. That 'proposition' ceases henceforth to be a law of nature, or even a proposition; it is reduced to a symbolic rule. This entire re-interpretation appears now as trivial and useless.—Any exposition which endeavors to obliterate such a fundamental difference is most dangerous."[60]

Further, the distinction between logical and descriptive signs, which offhand seems to be a semantic distinction, a distinction between logical and extra-logical, empirical designata, is also characterized formally, thus: a sentence containing only logical signs (expressions) is a sentence whose validity is determinate. Again, the distinction between variables and constants, and the various kinds of operators and connectives (conjunction, disjunction, implication) are formally defined.[61] Even the trans-

57

lation of a language into another can be interpreted in purely formal manner, without regard to meanings, as a many-one coordination of expressions or sentences or classes of sentences. Such a translation is adequate if and only if the corresponding expressions etc. in the two languages have the same logical content.

Finally even the concept "extensional", and its contrary "intensional", is defined with the help of the previously constructed definitions, by substituting in the customary definition of extensionality as truth-functionality for the concept "true", which is no genuinely syntactic concept, the concept "identity of logical content." Thus a proposition is extensional with respect to a component proposition if its logical content is invariant with respect to replacements of the component proposition with others of the same logical content. Now, Wittgenstein maintained that every proposition is a truth-function of elementary propositions, i.e. is extensional with respect to component propositions. But this does not hold for any possible language. For there are propositions which are not truth-functions of their component propositions, viz. intensional* propositions. Such are, e.g., propositions about states of affairs entertained, asserted or believed by people, like "many people have believed that Frederick Barbarossa continues to live in the mountain named Kyffhäuser". Here "Frederick Barbarosa" may be re-

---

Translator's note.—The author's terminology, while according with the earlier terminology of the *Logical Syntax*, is here at variance with the terminology more recently introduced by Carnap in *Meaning and Necessity*: there "p is intensional" is used in the sense of "the truth-value of p is invariant with respect to replacements of components of p with *L-equivalent* propositions", such that the intensionality of a proposition does not follow from its non-extensionality. In particular, propositions about propositional attitudes, like the below example, are non-extensional but not intensional, according to the recent terminology.

placed by the description "the emperor who drowned in the Saleph". But "that the emperor who drowned in the Saleph is still alive", is not the proposition which many people believed. Likewise modal propositions, which assert a necessity, an impossibility or the like, and propositions asserting a logical entailment, have been claimed as intensional propositions by Lewis[62] and others. Thus extensional and intensional propositions must both be recognized. However, Carnap believes that the assumption is justified that for every intensional language one can construct an extensional language into which the former is translatable (he still maintains this thesis of extensionality at present[63]; he only supplements it by a semantic definition of extensionality in which "identical logical content" is replaced by "equivalent in meaning").

While it was customary in the beginning to think, following Wittgenstein, of analyzing language *in general,* analysis has subsequently revealed that there is not just one language but several languages of varying forms. A language is determined by the kinds of signs it contains, the modes of sentence-formation and the transformation-rules for its sentences. All this is based on stipulations, and stipulations may be freely chosen. One may introduce signs with given meanings and admit or prohibit sentence-forms, as one sees fit. But the stipulations of formation- and transformation-rules must be made in such a way that they lead to correct results in accordance with the meanings assigned to the primitive signs. To this extent a given syntax cannot be freely chosen but is determined by the meanings of the signs. But even the latter stipulations can be freely adopted if one constructs first of all a symbolic system devoid of a fixed interpretation, a pure calculus, and only thereafter looks for a suitable interpretation of the primitive logical signs—and finds it too! It is possible to construct languages of diverse logical forms and of diverse logical extension, as was already shown in terms of the two languages constructed by Carnap. In the essay "Testability and Meaning"[64] he sketched a practically infinite series of possible languages.

It makes no sense to ask for justification, or to question the legitimacy of, linguistic forms. For there is no authority that could pronounce a unique judgment. There are no questions of truth or falsehood here, but only questions of stipulation and convenience. All one can do is to develop the consequences which a given stipulation, be it a prohibition or an admission, commits him to, and on this basis he can make a rational choice, i.e. a choice that will lead to his practical ends. One should not pronounce general prohibitions of sentence-forms or methods of deduction (the way Brouwer did it with respect to the law of the excluded middle, and Wittgenstein with respect to unrestrictedly universal statements), but should instead pay homage, in the logical analysis of language, to a principle of tolerance.[65] The significance of general syntax, as developed by Carnap, is elucidated in the face of the variety of possibilities of logical forms of languages. General syntax clarifies the essential nature of language qua formalized. It enables the reduction of languages of any form whatever to a common denominator, to recognize them as special illustrations of a universal structure and to state their characteristic properties and differences with precision.

It is likely that what led Carnap to the reduction of linguistic analysis to syntax was his acceptance of the verifiability principle of meaning which he wanted to apply to the statements of logical analysis too. At the Prague congress, Ingarden had objected[66] that on the basis of this definition of significance meta-linguistic sentences are either meaningless or non-sensical since they are in principle unverifiable, as, indeed, Wittgenstein also maintained at the end of his Tractatus.[67] For verification is feasible only in terms of observable physical facts; but the observable, physical aspects of language, inscriptions and sounds, so the argument went, are not what meta-linguistic sentences are about. For meaning is the essence of language. In order to answer this objection, Carnap had to endeavor to disassociate linguistic analysis from considerations of meaning and to direct it towards the observable shell of language, signs and their combination, syntax. Thus the statements of linguistic analysis would be verifiable and therefore meaningful.

Morris was the first one to assert that syntactic analysis is not the whole of linguistic analysis,[68] and in the meantime Carnap himself has recognized this limitation and spoken out to that effect. He now clearly sees the semantic dimension of language, whereas at first there existed for him in addition to the syntactic point of view in linguistic analysis only the psychological point of view which he now calls more generally "pragmatic". He has emancipated himself from the radical onesidedness of his original approach, where he thought that all problems of language and logic could be adequately treated syntactically, and is now doing justice to the semantic function of language. A systematic discussion of the latter is contained in his *Introduction to Semantics* (1942, 2nd ed., 1947).

But with this changed approach there has come a changed conception of the relationship of logic to syntax.

In the "Logical Syntax of Language" logic was represented as a branch of syntax and logical relations were syntactically interpreted. By defining the relation of logical consequence in purely syntactic terms, as a relation between the syntactic forms of sentences, he construed it as independent of the meanings of sentences. It is possible to ascertain whether the relation holds between two sentences on the basis of syntactic considerations alone, without reference to the meanings of the sentences. All logical concepts and relations can, and should be, expressed formally, including the logical contents of sentences. Formal logic is complete; there is no department of logic that can be dealt with only within a semantic framework; indeed, such a semantic framework was considered superfluous.

But since then Carnap has come to see, a point of fundamental importance, that the formalization of logic is but a secondary matter and that logic is based primarily on meaning, i.e., on semantic rules. C. I. Lewis already maintained that the concept of logical consequence differs[69] from the concept of implication, the if-then relation, as construed in the system of "Principia Mathematica", by Russell and Whitehead, and that it is in fact impossible to express the concept of logical consequence in this system.[70] Carnap himself has now made a fundamental amendment to his earlier view and holds that syntax alone is insufficient for the construction of logic. In the ultimate analysis, the distinction between logical and descriptive signs is definable only in terms of their meanings,[71] and similarly "logical truth", in contrast to "factual truth", means nothing else than "true on the basis of semantic rules." Syntax alone cannot guarantee that a given syntactic concept expresses the semantic relation it is intended to formalize, for this depends on the relations of the formalized system, the calculus, to the corresponding semantic system. It now appears to be entirely impossible to define syntactic concepts which can be interpreted *only* by unique, semantically defined, concepts. For this reason, Carnap has abandoned the syntactic definitions of logical concepts, as given in general syntax, at least in so far as they claim universal applicability (although the definitions are suitable for many calculi). In a new book, *Formalization of Logic* (1943, 2nd ed., 1947), he has undertaken a more complete formalization of logic by the method of calculus-construction.

(b) *Quasi-syntactic sentences*

In the representation of the syntax of a language there are always two languages involved: 1. the language whose syntax is described, the "object-language", and 2. the language by means of which the syntactic structure is described, the "syntax-language". The latter need not be a separate language, it might be a part of the object-language. In that case the statements of the syntax-language are logical statements of the object-language. But not all syntactic statements can be expressed in the object-language. For example, the concepts "analytic" and "contradictory" are not definable with the means of expression of a syntax-language constituting a part of the object-language, but only within a richer language.[72]

If the syntax-language is a part of the object-language, which is the usual case, the difference between the two languages must be clearly indicated. For a given designation (e.g. "Uno") might then mean either what is designated (the United Nations organization) or the designation itself (as, e.g., in: "Uno" is an abbreviation for "United Nations Organization"). If the designated object is itself a linguistic expression, as is the case with syntactic designations, then it is indispensable, in the interest of clarity, to refer to the linguistic expression as such by putting it between quotes or designating it by a name (as e.g. the letter-name "omega"). If an expression means itself (if it is "autonymous"), it is, strictly speaking, given a new meaning, for it is used as a designation for something new, viz. for signs, while it otherwise designated extra-linguistic objects. This distinction is clearly illustrated by the following example, given by Carnap (p. 109): W is an ordinal type; "W" is a letter; Omega is a letter; "Omega" is a word consisting of five letters. Frege was the first one to distinguish consistently between designations of objects and designations of designations, and his example was followed by the school of the Warsaw logicians. It happens not infrequently even today, however, that this distinction is neglected (as, e.g., by Heyting, Chwistek and others), which neglect leads to ambiguities.

Now, there obtain correspondences between properties of designated *objects* and properties of the latter's *designations*, of such a kind that if and only if a given property is predicable of a given object, the expression designating the object has a definite *syntactic* property. Thus, there corresponds to the object-sentence "five is a number" the syntactic sentence " 'five' is a number-word". If there corresponds to a sentence ascribing a property to an object a sentence which ascribes to a designation of that object a corresponding *syntactic* property, then the former sentence is translatable into the latter. Carnap calls a sentence of this kind "quasi-syntactic". Quasi-syntactic sentences admit of two interpretations.

64

They may be regarded as statements about a property
of an object, e.g. "five is a number"; the *designatum* of
the word "five" is thus included in a class of objects. Such
is the "material mode of speech". But they may also be
interpreted as statements about a syntactic property of
the *designation* of an object—"Five is a number-word"—,
where the expression ("five") designates, not an object,
but itself; thus it is used autonymously, which leads to
ambiguity. If instead of using quasi-syntactic sentences
one uses purely syntactic ones—" 'five' is a number-word",
where "five" is explicitly characterized as a designation—
then one employs the "formal mode of speech". The
latter is valuable because it unambiguously shows the
linguistic character of that which the assertion is about.

The class of quasi-syntactic sentences plays a significant role. It constitutes an intermediate domain between
pure object-sentences and purely syntactic sentences. If
we use the material mode of speech, quasi-syntactic sentences appear as object-sentences, but according to their
content they are really syntactic sentences, since they
refer to the *designations* of the objects which they seem
to talk about. The predicated properties are pseudo-ob-
ject-properties, properties which are "as it were disguised
as properties of objects", but "are syntactic properties
according to their meaning".[73]

His insight into this situation enables Carnap to
clarify all kinds of problems, by recognizing that what
is involved is a quasi-syntactic sentence. Thus the relation between implication and logical consequence is
clarified. Lewis, like Russell, regarded both implication
and logical consequence as relations between sentences,
and insofar as similar, and divided implications into
"strict" and "material". But implication and consequence

are totally different relations. Logical consequence is, indeed, a relation between sentences, but not so implication in the sense in which one event is said to imply another. For the latter is not about *sentences* connected with one another, but about what these sentences *designate*. The implication "if one starves, then one loses weight" says nothing about the two sentences, but refers to two kinds of processes. The relation of logical consequence, on the other hand, holds between sentences, not between processes (or events). Thus it is a syntactic relation. An implication asserting a causal relation between events is a synthetic statement. The "if"- and the "then"-sentence are connected simply as a matter of fact, and it is not possible to deduce the latter from the former. In the special case, however, where the relation of implication is not expressed by a synthetic but by an analytic statement, it coincides in logical content with the corresponding entailment-statement. But even so it does not become identical with the latter, since it still remains a statement in the object-language. Yet, in this case there exists a corresponding true statement in the meta-language expressing a syntactic relation, which is not the case if the statement of implication is factual, synthetic.

Similarly the true nature of modal concepts (necessary, contingent, possible, impossible) is clarified, by recognizing their quasi-syntactic character.[74] Traditionally, one distinguishes logical and real necessity, impossibility, etc. It is clear that the *logical* modalities express only the character of logical consequence, inconsistency etc. Yet, the same holds for the real modalities. They refer, indeed, to objects, asserting that a given state of affairs is necessary or possible. . . . But natural necessity is nothing else but the necessity of logical consequences of a law of nature. There are but facts in Nature. Organisms simply die, as a matter of fact. That they *have to* die, that death is *necessary* for every organism, is true only insofar as it is determined by biological laws, i.e. insofar as it *follows* from the latter. Should this not be the case, there would be no necessity for this event to occur; it would then be possible for organisms to be immortal. Thus "possible" only means "compatible with laws of nature". And similarly factual impossibility means nothing else but "incompatability with a law of nature". A perpetuum mobile is impossible because it contradicts the second law of thermodynamics. Contradiction is a purely logical relation, a relation between sentences. What corresponds to it in Nature is only non-existence; the self-contradictory simply does not exist. If facts or events are declared as necessary or contingent, possible or impossible, this can only mean that they are deducible from or incompatible with laws of nature. Modal sentences refer but apparently to relations between objects, in truth they are about relations between sentences. For they are translatable into purely syntactic sentences. The sentence "all organisms must die" corresponds to the syntactic sentence " 'all organisms will die' is an analytic sentence" (relatively to presupposed definitions and laws). The sentence "a perpetuum mobile is impossible" corresponds to the syntactic sentence " 'there is a perpetuum mobile' is P-contradictory". And the sentence "it is possible for an organism to be immortal" corresponds to the syntactic sentence " 'there are immortal organisms' is not P-contradictory". The sentence "star-constellations correlate with human fate just by chance" corresponds to the syntactic sentence

67

" 'star-constellations correlate with human fate' is neither analytic nor contradictory; that is, it is synthetic". Thus modal assertions are quasi-syntactic sentences.

Lewis insisted on the need for an intensional logic in order to accommodate the modal concepts (including the concept of logical consequence) (loc. cit.). One cannot express the concept of necessary validity of a statement in the system "Principia mathematica" (as object-language). For this reason Lewis emphasized that the modal concepts are non-extensional, i.e. require consideration of the meaning of sentences. Hence he introduced a new symbol standing for possibility as a primitive concept, on the basis of which he defined the concepts of impossibility and necessity. Afterwards students of his and others[75] constructed a special system of modal logic as an extension of the Russellian system.

Carnap, now, has shown that the modal concepts too can be formulated as logico-syntactic concepts, such that modal assertions may be interpreted as quasi-syntactic. What is of prime importance here, however, is their logical, not their syntactic character. Modal assertions, apparently about relations between states of affairs, are actually quasi-logical. Since logic is primarily based on semantics, modal logic should originally indeed be developed as a semantic system, a logic of meaning-relationships; as a matter of fact, such a construction of modal logic has been undertaken by Carnap in a new book Meaning and Necessity (1947). Nonetheless the fundamental clarification effected by the Logical Syntax of Language, that modal assertions are strictly speaking, not about relations between states of affairs, but about logical relations, remains unaffected. And to the extent that logic admits of syntactic formulation, it requires no special kind of logic. Every system of modal logic admits in that case of translation into a syntactic system. This does not rule out, to be sure, the construction of a special modal logic. But the latter is not indispensable, as one used to think.

Quasi-syntactic sentences result further from the predicative use of certain concepts which Carnap calls "universal predicates" or "universal words". Such terms designate a property or relation which is "predicable of all entities of a given type analytically" (p. 219). If in such a sentence, containing a universal predicate, we replace the subject with any other subject of the same type, we obtain again an analytic sentence, e.g.: a dog is a thing, the moon is a thing, or: seven is a number, zero is a number, and similarly for any other thing and for any other number. If, on the other hand, the subject is taken from another type, the resulting sentence is not even significant, e.g.: a lie is a thing, Caesar is a number. The following words are such "universal" words: thing, object, property, relation, fact, state, process, space, time, number, and others. They represent the conceptual or grammatical categories which are discriminated, by the logical grammarian, within the philological categories like substantives, adjectives, verbs etc.; they are the kind that was first recognized by Wittgenstein:[76] "syntactic categories".[77]

These "universal predicates" can be used in two ways. First, in order to characterize the syntactic type of an expression, for the sake of univocality, e.g. "the state of friendship" as distinct from "the relation of friendship", or in order to facilitate understanding or just for purposes of emphasis, e.g. "the process of heating". In this use the universal predicate is not autonomous, it functions merely as grammatical index to another expression, especially to a variable as represented by the words "a", "something", "every", "all". Since it is not definitely indicated what kinds of entities are substitutable for these variables, the type of admissible arguments in universal, existential and interrogative sentences should be specially characterized. For example, "for any number, if . . . , then . . .", or "there is a relation such that . . . ", or "at what time did . . .". Such sentences are genuine object-sentences, not quasi-syntactic sentences.

But, secondly, universal words may also be used as autonomous predicates, e.g. "five is a number", "friendship is a relation". In that case a *syntactic* predicate may be coordinated to the universal predicate, which applies to all *designations* of the given type, e.g. "five" is a numeral, "friendship" is a relative term. Here the universal word is a quasi-syntactic predicate and the sentences are quasi-syntactic.

(A sentence like "Caesar is a number" need not be meaningless. As Carnap has come to realize,[78] a sentence like "this stone thinks of Vienna" may be regarded as meaningless or as false, depending on the syntactic conventions of the language in which it occurs. Sentences of a universal predicate, but at the same time with a subject belonging to a different type than the type expressed by the predicate, are meaningless if the universal words form syntactic categories. But strictly speaking the difference between thing and property etc. is descriptive. In that case universal predicates do not necessarily represent syntactic categories. If they do not, then such sentences are false, not meaningless, and are not quasi-syntactic at all. In other words, they are quasi-syntactic only on the assumption that the universal words are incorporated into the syntactic rules.)

It is but apparently that quasi-syntactic sentences refer to extra-linguistic entities like numbers, properties, space etc.; in truth they are about designations, numerical expressions, predicates, spatial coordinates etc. They are merely "pseudo-object-sentences". Once one has acquired familiarity with quasi-syntactic sentences as such, one sees much more clearly what the questions at issue are and therewith the solutions often follow quite easily. This circumstance lends particular epistemological importance to quasi-syntactic sentences. Once they are translated into purely syntactic sentences, in other words, once the transition from the "material" to the "formal" mode of speech is made, there results not only a dispersion of misleading obscurities, but frequently even a dissolution of the problem. Thus the famous dictum of Kronecker's "God created the natural numbers; fractions and real numbers, however, are fabricated by man" admits of a more sober, yet more precise, formulation: the natural-number-signs are primitive signs, the expressions for fractions and real numbers are introduced by definitions (cf. later, p. 77).

As quasi-syntactic sentences are actually intended as syntactic sentences, they depend on the structure of a given language. Hence they should not be considered in isolation; rather one should specify in which language they are valid, in the customary language of science or in some other kind of language, or in any language. And for this reason such sentences cannot be considered true or false; all that can be asked is whether such linguistic conventions (including the consequences of the latter) as they exhibit are useful or not. The whole situation, therefore, differs from the situation in the case of object-sentences, the type of sentence they are readily confounded with.

Even some sentences which admit of semantic interpretation are regarded as quasi-syntactic by Carnap. The usual way of specifying the meaning of a word or sentence is to circumscribe the designated object or state of affairs by means of other words or sentences. Thus a relation of equivalence between sentences is produced. Consequently assertions about meanings can be formulated as assertions about syntactic relations between their designations. E.g., "day star" means the sun; that means, "the *word* 'day star' is synonymous with the *word* 'sun' ". "Synonymy" is a formal, syntactic concept, defined in terms of formal identity of content of sentences containing the respective designations. In this manner even relations between the meaning of different expressions and between the objects denoted by them admit of formal, syntactic formulation. For example, "evening star" and "morning star" differ in meaning but denote the same object. This fact is expressed by the syntactic sentence "the words 'evening star' and 'morning star' are synonymous, but not on the basis of their definitions alone, as e.g. 'baby cats' and 'kitten', but on the basis of experience". In the case of sentences, there corresponds to the statement "sentences S_1 and S_2 have the same meaning" the syntactic statement "S_1 and S_2 have the same logical content" (according to the definition of "logical content" on p. 52), again either on the basis of logic alone or only on empirical grounds.

But in the meantime Carnap has come to realize that statements about meanings are not properly quasi-syntactic, but have rather a semantic character.[79] Their formulation in terms of syntactic relations is a secondary matter, which would not be possible if it were not for a prior understanding of meanings. Semantic relations are primary. Moreover, the syntactic formulation of meaning is feasible only if the validity of the thesis of extensionality is presupposed. Expressions which have different meanings but denote the same object, and sentences which have different meanings but refer to the same fact, are neither quasi-syntactic nor quasi-logical, but purely semantic—a correction now made by Carnap himself. (loc. cit.). Similarly, he now interprets sentences with component sentences expressing a state of affairs believed or entertained or asserted by somebody, as well as sentences with component sentences functioning as indirect quotations, not as quasi-syntactic, nor as purely semantic but as pragmatic sentences about attitudes of interpreters, in whose formulation semantic concepts also are employed (loc. cit.).

In the *Logical Syntax of Language* Carnap regarded all non-extensional (intensional) sentences as quasi-syntactic. But the entire theory of quasi-syntactic sentences has been decisively modified through his insight into the importance of semantics, as expressed in *Introduction to Semantics* and *Meaning and Necessity*. Strictly speaking, it is *logical* relationships which provide a content for pseudo-object-sentences, the sort of sentences which are but apparently about objects. But, as Carnap now admits, logic is primarily based on semantics, not on syntax. Therefore pseudo-object-sentences are more aptly called "quasi-*logical*" instead of "quasi-*syntactic*". They should, in that case, be formulated first as semantic sentences and only afterwards be translated into syntactic sentences.[80] This is a clarification of fundamental importance. It blunts the edge of some of the objections raised against the capital which Carnap made of quasi-syntactic sentences, especially in connection with the role they play in philosophy. For in the *Logical Syntax of Language* Carnap established a close connection between philosophy and quasi-syntactic sentences, or between philosophy and syntax of the language of science.

The propositions and problems in any discipline concern either the latter's *subject-matter,* its properties and relations, or the logical relations of the *concepts, propositions and theories* which refer to the subject matter. Any sentence is necessarily either a genuine object-sentence or a syntactic sentence or, if it is a quasi-syntactic sentence, is transformable into a purely syntactic sentence. If the latter is not possible, then the sentence is devoid of scientific content altogether. Translatability into a syntactic sentence constitutes the touchstone of the meaningfulness of all those sentences which are neither genuine object-sentences nor purely syntactic sentences.

The application of this point of view to philosophy led to a new precise definition of philosophy as a science. Philosophy has no business with purely *factual* questions; for the latter belong to the special sciences, and a special domain of "facts" as the subject matter of transcendent metaphysics is out of the question. Thus philosophical questions can be only *logical* questions, questions of logical analysis of science.[81] In his general syntax Carnap demonstrated that all logical relations can be formulated formally, as relations concerning merely the "order and (syntactic) kinds of the signs of linguistic expressions", as syntactic relations. Accordingly Carnap arrived at the conclusion "that all significant problems of philosophy", at least the problems of non-metaphysical and non-normative philosophy, "belong to syntax".[82] Again it was Wittgenstein who was the first to express a similar conception of philosophy as regards its relation to the logic of science and to syntax (in the *Tractatus logico-philosophicus*), without, though, equating logic of science and syntax. According to Wittgenstein, syntactic rules alone are to be formulated without reference to meaning, while the propositions of the logic of science refer to the meanings of scientific concepts and propositions.

But philosophy is, as a rule, only rarely occupied with purely formal problems of calculus construction. Usually its questions are, especially in the context of philosophical foundation problems of the special sciences, questions apparently about *objects,* space, time, things, numbers etc. In truth, however, they are about concepts and propositions and theories, about the latter's logical character. Accordingly they are quasi-syntactic questions. Philosophy is logic of science and logic of science is syntax of the language of science. All philosophical questions are to be precisely formulated as syntactic questions. Carnap was, therefore, of the opinion that a great many philosophical questions, which are supposed to be about objects only owing to the influence of the material mode of speech, are actually quasi-syntactic questions, and can thus be clarified and solved through formulation in the formal mode of speech. Thus the opposition, in the controversy about the foundations of mathematics, between the formalist and the logicist interpretation of numbers can be resolved. According to the latter, natural numbers are defined as classes of classes of things, according to the former they are special, underived kinds of entities. Formally put, the mutually opposed theses are simply:

natural number-expressions are class-terms of the second
level, versus: natural number-expressions are expressions
of the zero level. And the controversy can be resolved by
pointing out that systems of arithmetic may be alternatively constructed on the basis of the first as well as on the
basis of the second definition (p. 227). Similarly, the
thesis of Wittgenstein, "the world is the totality of facts,
not of things", can be more clearly formulated in terms
of the corresponding syntactic thesis: science is a system
of sentences, not of names (p. 230).

Philosophical questions are usually formulated in
terms of "universal words" and accordingly speak about
kinds of objects. But this circumstance gives not infrequently rise to pseudo-questions about the nature of these
kinds of objects, of numbers, time, universals, etc. We
avoid such pseudo-questions if we replace the universal
words by corresponding syntactic expressions (numerical
expressions, time-coordinates, predicates). Such translation into sentences about designations often brings contradictions and nonsense into plain view. Assertions about
"what cannot be said", such as occur, following Wittgenstein, even within the Vienna Circle, thus turn into assertions to the effect that there are unspeakable objects and
facts, i.e. designations of undesignatable objects, and descriptions of undescribable facts; thus they show themselves as contradictions.

"In any domain of science whatsoever one must either
speak *in* sentences of that domain or *about* the sentences
of that domain".[83] Genuine sentences are either object-
sentences or syntactic sentences. However, they do not
form separate departments, special sciences on the one
hand, logic of science on the other hand; rather, both
kinds of sentences occur in the special sciences, where

assertions are made not only about the subject-matter but also about the concepts and propositions of the science, wherever logical relations form the subject of discussion; and both kinds of sentences are likewise to be found in the logic of science, where besides syntactic analysis we encounter also discussions about the psychological, sociological and historical conditions of linguistic usage. If the logic of science does its work in the field of the special sciences, it is with a different emphasis: logico-syntactic relationships are the focus of attention.[84]

But this definition of philosophy which restricts the latter to sentences about syntactic structure, i.e. about the "order and (syntactic) kinds of the signs of linguistic expressions" is much too narrow. Carnap has in the meantime recognized this limitation. He now defines the task of philosophy quite generally as "semiotic" (not to be confused with "semantic") analysis of the language of science and of the theoretical part of everyday language. "Semiotics" comprises the analysis of language along three dimensions: with regard to the *use* of language, i.e. from the pragmatic point of view, then with regard to the *meanings* of linguistic signs, from the semantic point of view, and with regard to the relations between signs *without* reference to their meanings, from the syntactic point of view. In philosophical discussions all three of these dimensions of inquiry are usually blended. In epistemology and philosophy of the sciences (philosophy of nature, foundations of mathematics) one is concerned, on the one hand, with the acquisition of linguistically formulated knowledge through perception, comparison, confirmation. To this extent such inquiries belong to pragmatics. They are psychological, sociological, historical, and thus empirical inquiries. On the other hand, there is a concern with logical analysis. If such analysis refers to the meanings of linguistic expressions, it moves in the field of semantics. It belongs to syntactics only if it is exercised in purely formal manner, as applied to a calculus.[85]

It follows, however, that it is no longer possible to say that philosophy deals above all with quasi-syntactic sentences, and that philosophical problems get dissolved, or at least clarified, by translation of these sentences into purely syntactic ones, as Carnap used to emphasize so heavily in the *Logical Syntax of Language*. For even if philosophical statements are not purely semantic, they are at any rate not quasi-syntactic but rather quasi-*logical*. Such statements must first be semantically formulated and only subsequently admit of syntactic formalization. It is impossible, therefore, to avoid reference to meaning, to relations between objects. Problems cannot in general be clarified by syntactic analysis, analysis of mere symbol-relations, transition from the material to the formal mode of speech.

On the contrary, linguistic formulations depend on the attained degree of clarity about objective relationships. If Kronecker's famous dictum about the natural and the extended kinds of numbers (see earlier, p. 71) seems to be immediately clarified by its translation into a statement about the difference between primitive signs and defined signs, this is, after all, only because Weierstrass and Meray gained insight into the reducibility of extended numbers to natural numbers. With reference to the alleged virtues of the formal mode of speech, elevating it above the material mode of speech, i.e. the advantages of syntactic over semantic formulations, Mill's criticism of Condillac's famous aphorism applies, "that a science is nothing, or scarcely anything, but *une langue bien faite;* in other words that the one sufficient rule for discovering the nature and properties of objects is to name them properly: as if the reverse were not the truth, that it is impossible to name them properly except in proportion as we already are acquainted with their nature and properties. Can it be necessary to say, that none, not even the most trivial knowledge with respect to Things, ever was or could be originally got at by any conceivable manipulation of mere names, as such; and that what can be learned from names, is only what somebody who used the names knew before?"[86] Indeed, Carnap himself says:[87] "A proposal concerning a syntactic reformulation of a certain point of the language of science is, to be sure, in principle a convention that may be freely chosen. But such a convention is practically useful and fruitful only if due attention is paid to the results, at the time available, of the empirical research carried on in the special sciences". The stipulation of primitive signs by which the other signs are to be defined is, at any rate, just such a syntactic reformulation (even though the circumstances determining such a choice in mathematics are not empirical discoveries).

But Carnap even frequently claimed sentences which cannot be properly interpreted as syntactic sentences, i.e. assertions about relations of designations, as quasi-syntactic. For the formulation of a quasi-syntactic sentence in the formal mode of speech is not just coordinated with its formulation in the material mode of speech, but this formulation brings out its proper meaning.[88] Thus the sentence "every tone has a definite pitch" cannot be properly translated into "every tone-name contains a pitch-name"[89] or the sentence "the originally given involves the sensory qualities, e.g. colors, smells and the like" cannot be properly translated into the syntactic sentence "the descriptive primitive signs are combined with names of sensations, e.g. color-names, smell-names and the like."[90] What is accomplished this way is merely a juxtaposition of assertions about objects with assertions about the latter's designations. The latter do not explicate the meanings of the former, but rather distort their true meanings; they talk about something else, about names of objects instead of objects. Sentences like "the moon is a thing", "five is a number" make assertions about classes of entities, while " 'moon' is a thing-word", " 'five' is a number-word" talk about the corresponding designations. It is obvious that the ontological problems vanish through this transition from the material to the formal mode of speech[91]—but not because they are thus revealed as pseudo-problems; it is rather because they are thus dodged. If we confine our discussion to numerical expressions instead of talking about numbers, there is naturally no such problem as what numbers are. But from the semantic point of view the problem remains as the question concerning the nature of the designata of numerical expressions. Carnap interpreted, in the L.S. d.Sp., the sentence "natural numbers are classes of classes of things" as a quasi-syntactic sentence, whose meaning is adequately expressed by the syntactic sentence "natural number-expressions are class-terms of the second level".[92] But one would hardly be doing justice to the conceptual accomplishment of Frege and Russell, were one to reduce it to a mere linguistic convention, an alternative to a convention like "numerical expressions are expressions of the zero level".[93] Following Carnap's own warning against the "careless" use of the word "meaningless",[94] we may add a word of caution against the careless use of the word "pseudoproblem". It is all too easy to dispose of inconvenient questions as meaningless or "pseudo", by shifting the discussion from the entities and their relations to their designations—which is something else.

If Carnap, in his earlier conception of language, and partly also the Vienna Circle, cannot easily be defended against the charge that their position was the most radical kind of nominalism, or mere vocalism, this is largely due to the exclusive adoption of the syntactic point of view and neglect of the semantic point of view. Again and again we find formulations suggesting that concepts and assertions are nothing else but their verbal expressions, as though their meanings had fallen into oblivion. For example, "names of physical objects (e.g. the word 'moon') are reducible to sense-data predicates".[95] After all, it is concepts that are reducible, not names (or words).

This vocalism is conspicuous above all in their conception of logic and mathematics. The latter "consist of nothing but conventional rules concerning the use of symbols. And the symbols of logic and mathematics do not, therefore, designate objects, but serve only for the symbolic formulation of those rules".[96] " '5+7=12' is no assertion at all, it is a rule which permits us to transform a sentence containing the symbols '5+7' into an equivalent sentence containing the symbol '12'. It is a rule governing the use of symbols".[97] "The sentences of arithmetic are composed of symbols of such and such kinds in such and such ways; such and such transformation-rules are valid". "Once we employ the formal mode of speech, in which we do not speak of 'numbers' at all but only of 'numerical symbols', the pseudo-question disappears what kind of entities numbers are."[98] Mathematics treats only of the manner "in which we wish to speak about objects,[99] and thus only of language." According to this view numbers are nothing but numerical symbols and number-words and these signs designate nothing but their own rules of manipulation. This holds, however, only for the purely formalistic reconstruction of mathematics, not for the logistic and intuitionist reconstructions. The propositions of logic and mathematics reduce to mere series of symbols only if they are formalized, in a calculus. But besides the calculus there is also a semantic system, as Carnap has, indeed, clearly shown since those early days. There can be no doubt about the fact that logic and mathematics are not concerned with empirical facts; but it does not follow that they treat merely of symbols. Their symbols too have meanings, designate something. A number, e.g. 3, does not simply consist in the number-word or numeral; what both designate is a definite multiple of unity; 1+1+1, brought into synthetic unity. For this reason an assertion about a number cannot be replaced with an assertion about the number-word. And the meaning of the sentence "five is a number" is not, therefore, adequately expressed by " 'five' is a number-word".

Logic likewise confines itself to mere symbols only in formalized logistics. But the stipulation of the rules of logic is based on definite meanings of the logical constants. Thus the tables of the truth-functions correspond to the meanings of the sentential connectives ("and", "or" etc.). These meanings may either be defined by specified relations of truth-values or they may be presupposed as bases for the specification of the kinds of truth-functions. Yet, all these objections hit but a standpoint that has been superseded. In his recent works Carnap has overcome the onesidedness of the merely syntactic point of view and done full justice to the semantic angle. In an appendix to *Introduction to Semantics* (p. 246 f.) , he explicitly calls attention to the modification of the *Logical Syntax of Language* thus necessitated, and abandons the restriction of philosophy to syntax of the language of science.

The achievement of Carnap's *Logical Syntax of Language* is best characterized by the words dedicated to it by one of the most eminent logicians of the present time, Joergensen, in a review:[100] "This new book of Carnap's is surely one of the most important publications in the philosophical literature of our time . . . It will, so it may be conjectured, be considered in future times as one of the landmarks on the arduous road of genuinely scientific philosophy".

B. EMPIRICISM

I. THE CONSTITUTION-SYSTEM OF EMPIRICAL CONCEPTS

The meaning of a word, or of signs in general, can be specified by producing other words (signs) whose meanings are already determined. This is the usual method of meaning-specification by definitions. But there are limits imposed upon definability owing to the fact that eventually the meanings of the words (signs) used to define must in turn be indicated, since otherwise one would move in a circle of mere words (signs) . Words (signs) must be connected with something other than words (signs). This is done by coordinating the sign to what is designated through direct presentation of the designated, through "ostensive definition". It is not just things or processes which are thus presentable but also situations, e.g. situations in which "yes" or "here" or "but" should be used. However, it is only the immediately given which is capable of being presented. Consequently it must be, if not sensible, capable of being experienced. Thus words (signs) acquire on the one hand a *subjective* meaning, designating a qualitative content, on the other hand an *intersubjective* meaning capable of being communicated in that they designate but the structure of the given, as was explained earlier (p. 41 f.) .

Accordingly the given constitutes the basis of all word-meanings; this is a central thesis of empiricism. Meanings must ultimately be founded upon presentation of the designated, and therefore all meanings must ultimately be reducible to the given, which alone is capable of presentation. And this means that all conceptual meanings can be constructed on the basis of experienced data alone.

A magnificent attempt at such construction of concepts was made by Carnap in his book "Der logische Aufbau der Welt", 1928. His "constitution-system", however, claims to be no more than a sketch, not a final system; it is intended to serve only as an illustration of the task of such a systematic construction. Above all it is intended to show the method to be employed for such a construction and "to prove that it is in principle possible to construct a unitary system of all scientific objects (concepts)" (p. 209) . That which the axiomatic method achieved in such brilliant style for the *propositions* of individual disciplines, viz. their logical deduction and thus reduction to their logical foundations, Carnap has attempted to do for the *concepts,* specifically the principal classes of concepts, of the whole of science.

To "constitute" a concept means to establish a general rule for replacing any assertion containing this concept by assertions containing other concepts. This is what a "constitutional definition" of a concept is. Not all concepts are definable, but only concepts belonging to higher levels of complexity. It is the meanings which can only be presented, through experience, which are the indefinable primitive concepts, constituting the basis of the former. Accordingly any assertion about entities of higher levels must be transformable into assertions which contain exclusively primitive concepts and logical, i.e. formal, concepts.

The constitution of concepts occurs in steps, by using the concepts first constituted in terms of the primitive ones to constitute further concepts, which are in turn used to constitute more complex concepts, etc. A constitution of this kind builds concepts upon one another in accordance with their order of presupposition. Thus, "acceleration" is defined in terms of the concepts "increase of velocity" and "time"; and "velocity" in turn is defined in terms of the concepts "displacement" and "time". In order to determine *which* concepts are presupposed by others, on a higher level, Carnap determines which concepts are epistemologically prior. The hierarchy of concepts thus constituted is accordingly constructed in conformity to the epistemological order. This requires scrutiny of the various kinds of concepts with regard to their reducibility, which latter results from the scientific knowledge had about the relevant subject-matter. "The constitution-system is a rational reconstruction of the entire construction of reality, which is, in the actual process of acquiring knowledge, achieved intuitively", (p. 139). The goal, then, is a logical family-tree of concepts on the basis of phenomenal data.

The phenomenal data of each person consist in

Methodological Solipsism [handwritten marginal note]

nothing but his own experiences. For knowledge of other minds is possible only on the basis of one's *own* perceptions of the expressions of other minds. For this reason the basis of the constitution-system is composed of solipsistic data ("eigenpsychische" basis), i.e. data pertaining to but *one* self, and indeed only conscious, not unconscious, data. Carnap called this point of view "methodological solipsism". This designation has been misunderstood as involving a metaphysical commitment: as though the sole reality of *one* self were presupposed, an imputation explicitly repudiated by Carnap (p. 86). In point of fact, all that is meant is that the constitution-basis is restricted to actual phenomenal data. But it is illegitimate to designate phenomenal data on the epistemologically primitive level as "solipsistic", i.e. as "psychical" and as "mine", as belonging to my self. For the self is not encountered in the "primordial situation of givenness", and "self" presupposes as a contrast "you", and the psychical presupposes as a contrast the physical. It follows that the data of experience, which we start from, cannot be characterized as "mine" until after the constitution of these concepts, and so on a higher level of the constitution-system. This characterization results only later, according to the sphere of entities within the system to which the elements belong. Primordially it is nothing but the factually given, neither "mine" nor "psychical" but something wholly neutral. After all, any concept in terms of which it could be described requires first of all construction on the basis of the given. In the construction of a constitution-system basis and logical construction must be clearly distinguished.

It is not discrete, qualitative elements, elements of sensation, which Carnap presupposes as data of experience—in this respect he differs from the neo-positivism of Mach and Ziehen. For these elements are the products of high abstraction, of a complicated conceptual construction. It is totalities which are actually experienced: perceptions, thoughts, feelings, desires, moods woven into one another as a unified whole, an ever specific *quale*. It is the continuous stream of experiences, ever changing, which is primordial.

Analysis consists in the search for parts within a complex, division of the complex into its elements. Analysis proper of the experientially given into parts is impossible since the given is not composed of real parts. Carnap proposes a different method for its conceptual construction, a method which is properly speaking synthetic. It is possible to discriminate positions within the stream of experience, and then relations may be discovered between these positions, e.g. that one position resembles another in a certain respect. All that can be said about the stream of experience is that one position stands in a certain relation to another. What Carnap calls "elementary experiences" are not qualitative elements in the psychological sense but only terms of relations picked out of the stream of experience, point-like and devoid of properties. Assertions about elementary experiences can be only about their *relations,* not about their *qualitative* aspects, since concepts referring to the latter must first be constituted. Visual or auditory perceptions are not parts of the stream of experience but are first abstracted from the latter by means of relatings and comparisons. They are not originally given but emerge only as the result of abstraction by means of a similarity-relation to other positions in the stream of experience, and they are discriminated within the latter in the same way in which

a tone can be discriminated within a triad, i.e. only
through its resemblance to other tones. They are abstract products of concept-formation just like pitch.
They represent but similarity-relations between positions
of the stream of experience. Accordingly the basis of the
constitution-system does not consist of primitive classes
of elements, but of primitive relations on which the order
of experiences depends. It is the primitive relations, not
the primitive elements, which are represented by the
undefined primitive concepts. On the contrary, the primitive elements are first constructed by means of the primitive relations as their terms.

Carnap believes—as long as the constitution-system
is not completely constructed he cannot assert this with
finality—that a single primitive relation suffices for its
construction: similarity between elementary experiences;
and since this similarity is recognized by comparison of a
present elementary experience with a past, and thus remembered one, it is similarity-*remembrance* which constitutes the primitive relation. In terms of the latter, kinship-relations between elementary experiences are determined, and on the basis of these relations there result
similarity-circles which are identical with classes of qualities that constitute the foundation of the similarities
holding between positions. These similarity-circles are
conceptual substitutes for the parts which usually result
from division. They perform the same conceptual function, they function as "quasi-elements" and the described
procedure as "quasi-analysis".

"Quasi-analysis" consists in the fitting of an elementary experience into a system of kinship-relations on the
basis of similarity-remembrance in such a way as to pre-
serve the unity of the experience. In this way "quasi-ele-

ments" can be discriminated within an elementary experience. The relation between the elementary experiences is either that of partial identity in a certain respect or that of merely partial similarity. In the first case, the similarity-circles are mutually exclusive, in the second case there is multiple overlapping. In the first case the similarity-circles are themselves quasi-elements, in the second case the latter must first be abstracted from the similarity-circles, "as the largest sub-classes which are not divided by the overlap of similarity-circles" (p. 101). In this manner one obtains similarity-classes, further relations between such classes, again classes of such classes and classes of such relations and even higher classes and relations of this sort. Thus there result ever narrower similarity-domains and by this method one is led to the formation of ever more specific concepts. All quasi-elements are thus the result of abstraction, and all determinate properties and entities are logical constructions out of the totality of experiences.

The first result of comparative quasi-analysis are classes of elementary experiences which are partially similar to one another, similarity-circles. From the latter one may select sub-classes, "quality-classes", which represent qualities of sensations or of feelings. Two quality-classes are similar if every element of the one class is partially similar to every element of the other class. If two quality-classes are such that there is a series of qualities progressing always from a given quality of the one class to a similar quality of the other class, then the two quality-classes belong to the same sense-field (the visual or auditory field or the field of temperatures, or the field of feeling-qualities). The class of quality-classes resembling one another in the indicated fashion is a "sense-class". Within a sense-class the order of qualities with respect to their similarities is determined in terms of their neighborhood-relations. The latter has a definite number of dimensions by which the sense-field in question is characterized in a purely formal way, without reference to qualitative content. For the visual sense the dimensionality is five, since colors have three dimensions (chroma, saturation and brightness) and the visual field extends in two dimensions. Finally, components of qualities can be constructed as classes of quality-classes of a given sense-field: quality in the narrower sense, intensity, locality-signs in the case of the sense of touch, directedness of feelings etc.

It is evident, then, that the conceptual construction here does not proceed, as is customary in psychology as well as in epistemology, from the most specific, sensations, to the ever more abstract and general, to qualities as classes of sensations, then to sense-fields etc., but on the contrary: first we have the construction of the most general classes of quasi-elements and only on the basis of these the more special classes are constructed: from quality-classes we proceed to sense-classes and only thereafter to sensations. A sensation is "an ordered pair of an elementary experience and a quality--class to which the experience belongs" (p. 130). Thus colors, which have a maximum of specificity, are constructed at the very end. Positions in the visual field are constructed as classes of quality-classes belonging to the visual field, and neighborhood-positions as classes of positions in the visual field. On this basis, equi-colority of neighboring positions is constituted as a relation of quality-classes of the visual sense, and then colors are defined as classes of equi-colored positions. This clumsy detour is inevitable if one wishes to be clear about the logical presuppositions of definability. If one cannot simply presuppose the concept of a Machean sensation-element (e.g. blue) as indefinable primitive concept, as it is already a product of abstraction, then more general concepts ("color") are needed for its definition, and the definition of the latter requires in turn more general concepts ("visible") , until one finally arrives at some ultimate, most general concept ("stream of experience").

The visual field is constituted as the two-dimensional order of neighborhood-positions. Thus the first instance of spatial order, that of the visual field, has been constructed. In terms of similarity-remembrance it is also possible to abstract *temporal* order of elementary experiences, since the remembered element is characterized as earlier relatively to the present element, and this enables a preliminary construction of temporal order—preliminary since it still contains gaps which will have to be filled later by means of inferences from regularities.

It is in this manner that *solipsistic* concepts are constructed. All these constitutional definitions are formulated in various ways, in four "languages": first, in logistic symbolism, for the sake of precision; secondly in the ordinary language into which the language of symbolic logic is translatable; thirdly, in realistic language in order to enable material understanding of the definitions in terms of recognition of familiar objects, which in turn enables tests of material adequacy; fourthly, as operational precepts for artificial constructions, which serve the purpose of elucidating the formal structure of constitutions of entities and to enable tests of the formal adequacy of the constitutions. However, the constitution of the higher levels, the levels above the solipsistic level, is indicated in terms of one language only, ordinary language, since it can only be sketched, not rigorously carried out.

The first of these higher levels is the *perceptual world*. It is not subjective visual space, but rightaway objective physical space, the space of perceivable objects, and objective time, which are constituted as its foundation. In this context the specific qualities of the spatial and the temporal are neglected; space and time are constituted in terms of "world-points" as the four-dimensional order of such "points". A world-point is determined by its co-ordinates (three spatial and one temporal co-ordinate) as a quadruplet of numbers. World-points with the same temporal coordinate are "simultaneous". The class of all mutually simultaneous world-points constitutes a "space-class". A "world-line" is a continuous "curve such that there corresponds to every value of the time-coordinate one and only one world-point" (p. 167). Thus the space-time order is nothing but a system of numerical relations (between coordinates).

To world-points colors are attributed (as visual quality-classes) and on their basis "visual objects" are defined as classes of world-points with invariant neighborhood relations during an extended time-interval, within a bundle of world-lines. Similarly tactual quality-classes which agree in their local reference are attributed to world-points, and thus there emerge tactual objects and, by combination with the former, things at once visible and tangible.

The most important tactual-visual-thing is "my body". The body acquires a closed surface only through ascription of tactual qualities besides visual qualities (colored points), since a large part of its surface is only touchable, not directly visible. It is only on the basis of its conceptual constitution that further specializations of the sense-fields, and on the basis of the latter the objects of the perceptual world, can be constituted. The sense-organs admit of constitutional characterization as parts of the body; and in terms of the concept "sense-organ" the concepts of the remaining senses (hearing, smell, taste) can in turn be constituted.

The qualities referring to these senses are predicable of world-points just like visual and tactual qualities, and thus the list of properties of perceptual objects is completed. But not all qualities are predicated of them in the same way. "There are qualities pertaining to certain senses (e.g. the sense of equilibrium, the kinesthetic sense, the organic sensations) which are hardly, if at all, predicable of definite worldlines or bundles of such, that is to say, of visual objects. However, no sharp boundary can be drawn between predicable and non-predicable sense-qualities" (p. 177), in the sense of the traditional distinction between primary and secondary qualities. Just the way sugar is characterized as sweet because it produces taste-sensations of this kind, so a melody may be called "gay", a letter "sad", a deed "outrageous", since such feelings are produced by them. It is only because the feelings produced by the same objects vary in degree from person to person more strongly than most sensations, and because consequently predications of the corresponding dispositions upon the same objects by different people lead to contradictions, that they are usually, though not in the child's thinking nor in lyrical poetry, attributed to the inner world instead of to the external world.

In order to complete the construction of the perceptual world, Carnap makes some additions of far-reaching significance. He introduces unseen colored points and untouched tactual points besides the seen and touched points, by ascribing to certain points of his coordinate-space visual and tactual qualities, and he undertakes, generally speaking, to attribute certain sense-qualities to points of a space-time domain which lack them, by analogy to the corresponding points of another space-time domain which overlaps considerably with the former. In realistic language this means: if we perceive again a spatial part of an object already perceived once, without however perceiving the remaining parts, we postulate that those parts of the object which correspond to the previously perceived parts of the object still exist in the unperceived spatial region—unless other inferences contradict this assumption; and if the larger temporal segment of a process already perceived once is perceived again, we postulate—in the absence of contrary evidence—that the process developed analogously in the remaining, unperceived, temporal parts. The meaning of this procedure is clear: it amounts to a constitution of momentarily unobserved parts of things and processes, such as hind-surfaces, the inside of objects, effects.[101] These predications by analogy serve to make postulates of substantiality and causality applicable, or putting it the other way around: "The two categories of causality and substantiality signify the application of one and the same constitution-by-analogy to diverse coordinate-directions" (p. 180).

The attribution of sense-qualities to the points of the four-dimensional coordinate-space results in the conceptual constitution of the perceptual world. Through elimination of sense-qualities and predication of numerical values of physical state-variables there results the *physical world*. This latter constitution creates a domain for which mathematically formulated laws can be established, enabling the deduction of future states from initial states; a domain which is entirely intersubjective while the perceptual world is not free from inconsistency owing to variations from person to person. There exists, however, a reciprocal correspondence between the physical and the perceptual world, a one-one correspondence between the physical world-points and the points of the perceptual world, a one-many correspondence between qualities and values of state-variables in that definite qualities correspond to the values of physical state-variables at a definite world-point, while a definite quality at a given world-point determines uniquely only a *class* of values of a state-variable.

The next higher level of the constitution-system is that of *other* consciousness. Within the perceptual world it is possible to constitute the class of "other people" as a subclass of the class of physical objects on the basis of the analogy between certain physical objects in the environment and "my body". Further, it is possible to co-ordinate to the class of "my" mental states a class of perceivable physical states of my body which often occur simultaneously with the mental states, and thus to constitute the "relation of expression". It is also possible to constitute the concept "signifying expression" (though with some difficulties) on the basis of the relation of signification, which serves as the foundation for the understanding of signs produced by others for purposes of communication. It is on the basis of these constructions that the concept of other consciousness is constitutionally defined. This concept means private mental events projected into the body of another person. For experiences of another person, however they may differ from one's own experiences, can be constructed only out of quasi-elements of one's own experiences. The expressive symptoms of mental states of another person can be interpreted only on the basis of what one is himself acquainted with. And the only way unowned mental states* can be known is through the mediation of a body. These predications are expanded into predications of entire sequences of experiences on the basis of psychological laws of co-existence and succession which have been discovered by reflection upon co-existences and sequences of elements of experience discernible in one's own experiences. Thus "the solipsistic basis is not abandoned" even during the constitution of other consciousness (p. 194).

A new constitution-system, the world of other people, can be constructed out of the experiences of other people in exactly the same way as the previous constitution-system was constructed out of owned experiences, viz. with the help of a primitive relation between unowned experiences called "similarity-remembrance (of the other person)", and by means of the same forms and steps of constitution. This constitution-system, however, is but a sub-system of the solipsistic constitution-system which mirrors the latter according to a certain analogy. This is possible because both are incomplete systems. For this reason one can constitute for every element of one system a corresponding element of the other system, "provided this system is worked out sufficiently" (p. 198). We have here an exact representation of how the thought of an

---

Translator's Note: Unfortunately there is no adjective in English that would serve as synonym for the philosophical German adjective "fremd-psychisch"; hence the circumlocution "unowned mental state" is used, which is throughout meant in the sense of "mental state unowned *by me*", not in the sense of "mental state unowned by any mind".

objective external world is conceptually developed in a single consciousness simultaneously with the thought of the inner worlds of fellow humans.

An extensive, though incomplete, analogy holds between the total system and the sub-system referring to the fellow human, i.e. between my world and your world. To the *originally* constituted concepts of the self, of perceptual objects, of the physical space-time world, of other consciousness there correspond generally analogous concepts in the *derived* constitution system. However, this correspondence does not hold in detail. The physical object "my body", contained in the constitution-system of a certain *fellow human* as experienced by him, is by no means identical with the object "body of fellow human NN" in the *total* constitution-system. There are more such "common", i.e. corresponding, objects in the two constitution-systems which are partially dissimilar because their relations to the fellow human's body differ from their relations to my body. But a one-one correspondence can be established between the physical world in the total system and the physical worlds in each sub-system pertaining to a given fellow human: the same space-time relations hold between corresponding world-points, and indirectly, through attribution of qualities to world-points, identical qualitative relations likewise hold. Thus we obtain an *inter-subjective* coordination. The concept of the "same" object, experienced and known by myself as well as others, can be defined as the class of intersubjectively coordinated objects. So far the concept of intersubjectivity has been applied only to the various physical worlds. But it is equally applicable to the psychical worlds. An unowned mental state which is, in the total system, ascribed to the body of a given fellow human, corresponds to the unowned mental states which are ascribed to the analogous bodies in the sub-systems.

By filling in empty places in the various constitution-systems on the basis of predications in other constitution-systems, a thoroughgoing, universally one-one, intersubjective coordination between the constitution-systems is made possible, and thus an intersubjective world is constituted. Properties of intersubjective objects which correspond in all constitution-systems, and assertions about them are accordingly intersubjectively transmissible, while properties which occur only in this or that constitution-system, and assertions about them, are subjective.

The next higher level of constitution, the last one, is represented by the concepts referring to *social* or cultural phenomena. Here Carnap confines himself to a demonstration, in terms of illustrations, of the *possibility* of their constitution, without going into its detailed forms. The cultural objects are constituted on the basis of the psychical objects. This does not convict the procedure of psychologism, for the entities on a higher logical level always constitute a novel domain. Primary cultural objects are those which do not already presuppose cultural objects for their constitution. They are constituted "on the basis of those psychical processes through which they appear", on the basis of their "manifestations", like e.g. greeting through lifting one's hat. It is on the basis of the primary ones, that the higher, remaining, cultural phenomena are to be constituted, such as those of society, of economics, of the legal order, etc. Values, on the other hand, are not constituted on the basis of cultural phenomena or of the phenomena of other consciousness but out of solipsistic value experiences, analogous to the constitution of physical objects out of perceptual experiences. Such value experiences are feelings of duty, responsibility, conscience, moral sentiments etc. This constitution of values does not involve psychologism, no more than the constitution of things.

Finally even the concept of empirical *reality,* in contrast to metaphysical reality, is constitutionally defined. Metaphysical reality, in the sense of existence independent of consciousness, does not admit of constitution. It is the mark of the empirically real, as contrasted with the unreal (dreams, fiction), that every real entity has a position in the temporal order, is intersubjective or at least is an element in the constitution of an intersubjective entity, and that it belongs to a comprehensive, rational system. Thus physical objects are real "if they are constituted as classes of physical points which lie on connected bundles of world-lines and which are fitted into the four-dimensional total system of the physical space-time world" (p. 237). And psychical objects are real if they fit into the psychical system of a self. Thus the difference between reality and unreality is constitutionally defined, entirely on the solipsistic basis without presupposing some sort of transcendental reality.

Insight into the constitution of concepts leads to many philosophical clarifications. Thus, it becomes clear what the difference between the *individual* and the general is. Since all concepts are constituted as classes or relations of elementary experiences, it follows that there are no properly individual concepts but only general concepts. What individualizes objects is their temporal, and in some cases also spatial, determination, i.e. their position in a temporal, and possibly also spatial, order. Universals, on the other hand, constitute the field of other kinds of ordering relations. The difference between spatio-temporal ordering relations and other kinds of ordering relations is rooted in the fact that there exist two different kinds of relations between quality-classes, as for example in the case of the visual sense, spatial coincidence and equi-colority. The first relation is the foundation of visual-field-order, and thus indirectly of spatial order. The second relation is the foundation of the qualitative order of colors in the spectrum. A property distinguishing the first relation from the second is the formal or logical property that different *equi-positional* quality-classes cannot ever belong to the same elementary experience while *equi-colored* quality-classes may. This is the ultimate basis of individuality.

Again, the concept of logical *identity* now admits of precise formulation. This concept is involved in the question "under what conditions are two different designations, designations of the same object?". The criterion of such identity consists in the mutual substitutability of the designations; that is, if alternative substitutions of the designations for the variable of a sentential function yield sentences of identical truth-value. In most cases of assertions of identity, however, the word "same" is not meant to apply to the mentioned object (e.g. this butterfly) *qua* individual, but to its kind (this species *butterfly*), and thus to an entity of higher level. If taken in this sense, "identity" is an exact concept, the concept just defined. If, on the other hand, identity is predicated of the object qua individual, then we do not have to do with identity proper but only with equivalence-relations (similarity with respect to some property, continuity or intersubjective coordination). This is but improper identity.

Again, by separating the logical problem from the metaphysical problem, an unambiguous formulation of *psycho-physical* dualism and of the mind-body relationship becomes possible. Since the various kinds of constituted entities are, strictly speaking, nothing but different forms of ordering a unitary kind of quasi-elements of the stream of experience, the two spheres of entities, the physical and the psychical, are by no means the only forms of order, but besides them we have others: the biological, the cultural objects, and values. Within the constitution-system there reigns, therefore, not a dualism but a pluralism of constituted kinds of entities.

As regards the problem of mind-body interaction, Carnap adopts the hypothesis of psycho-physical parallelism: to every mental event there corresponds a simultaneous physiological event in the central nervous system with which the former is regularly correlated. From the standpoint of constitution this means that there are two parallel series of quasi-elements of a sequence of experiences (those observations by which the relationship is ascertained). Such parallelism of quasi-elements, however, is not confined to the physical and psychical; it likewise appears in other series of elements, e.g. "whenever a body has a definite visual shape it also has simultaneously a definite tactual shape" (p. 234). Psychophysical parallelism is not fundamentally different from those other parallelisms, it is not any more problematic than the latter. The question how such parallelism arises, how it is to be explained, could be raised in exactly the same sense for all of them. This question, however, lies beyond the field of science, it belongs to metaphysics where it is answered in terms of postulates about reality. Science can only ascertain the brute fact of parallelism, between whatever kinds of elements it may hold.

The discussed constitution-system of concepts is no

more than an attempt, a first sketch—a fact deliberately emphasized by its author and by no means surprising if one considers the tremendous difficulty of the task. Nevertheless the fundamental task, which is to clarify the principle and method of definition of concepts, has thus been actually tackled. It is an old postulate that all concepts should be reducible to inner and external perception, to immediate impressions. It has been proclaimed by Locke and Hume, who laid it down as the foundation of their epistemology. But such a reduction had never been actually undertaken. It is Carnap who actually made the bold attempt, by endeavoring to show the definitional construction of at least the fundamental concepts on the sole basis of experiences. He did it with outstanding clarity and thoroughness, which lends fundamental importance to his attempt in spite of its incompleteness. He surely does not merit such a contemptuous judgment as Gerh. Lehmann passed on him in his 'Deutsche Philosophie der Gegenwart", 1943 (p. 299): "One can hardly fail to see the naiveté of the pretense to constitute the world with such (inadequate) means".

An acute, fundamental and incisive critique of the theory of constitution has been given by Kaila,[102] of which Carnap himself said:[103] "A monograph, like the one under discussion, which shows a thorough and clear insight into the connections between the problems, is a valuable contribution because of the competent and acute criticisms it contains"—in contrast to other criticisms of which Kaila says (p. 29) "It is hardly worth the effort even to pay attention to such high-handed objections as those that were brought forth by Kroener".[104] What Kaila considers as the fundamental error of Carnap's theory is that the constitution of concepts begins epistemologically too early, in such a way that it lacks the necessary pre-suppositions for such constitution. Its basis consists of the cross-sections through the stream of experience, which Carnap takes as qualitative totalities devoid of internal multiplicity and differentiation in order to avoid the old atomistic conception according to which there are aggregates of psychical elements. This approach, however, conflicts with modern Gestalt psychology which has recognized the structured nature of the data of experience. If all descriptions of the data of experience are posterior to the constitution of concepts, then all internal differentiation of these data is only the result of their conceptual analysis. In that case the internal multiplicity of the data, which is presupposed by the possibility of ascertaining relations of similarity, is lacking. Similarities, in that case, could hold only between experienced totalities as totalities, but there would be no similarities and no internal differentiations for the process of comparison and relating called "quasi-analysis". Analyzable internal multiplicity of the data of experience constitutes a necessary presupposition for this procedure, and the constitution of concepts through quasi-analysis can occur only on a higher level.

Thus subjective time cannot be regarded as a logical construction but its differentiation into present, past and future must be presupposed before constitution begins. Also the *sense* of a relation, i.e. the fact that its terms are not simply interchangeable, derives, according to Kaila, from the experience of temporal directedness. In replying to Kaila's critique,[105] Carnap dulls the edge of this objection by saying that what is really in question is not the direction of a relation but only the way the relation is designated, i.e. a way of symbolizing the relation so as to make the diversity of the term-designations and their relative positions recognizable.

Similarly, perceptual (or presentational) space does not admit of quasi-analytic constitution because it is unlimited, lacks boundaries, in other words, every point in it has a continuous three-dimensional environment. All that is at our disposal, however, to serve as constitution-basis is a limited number of distinguishable positions with spatial character; hence any constituted space would have to have a boundary, a beginning and an end. If the basis consists of a finite protocol of experiences, then unlimited systems capable of indefinite expansion, like space and time, indeed like the whole of reality, cannot be constituted. To this objection Carnap replies that one can easily construct infinite aggregates out of a finite number of elements, such as the infinite sequence of numerals which is formed out of the ten digits.

A further objection raised by Kaila is this. There is a fundamental difference, overlooked by Carnap, between "real" manifolds, like space and time, and "ideal" manifolds like that of the colors. A color, considered as a position in the order of the spectrum, is nothing but a class; a position in the visual field, however, or in space-time order in general, is not a class but something individual. Yet, Carnap constitutes even positions in the visual field as sub-classes of classes of elementary experiences. According to his theory of constitution, all multiplicity is but conceptual abstraction from the stream of experience; it consists in nothing but classes of similarities within the latter, and there exist only formal differences, differences in the way of grouping classes, into classes of classes, classes of relations, relations between classes etc. Consequently all the constitution-system can do is to display relations between similarities within the stream of my experiences; there is no room in it for novelty, everything is just a complicated ordering and re-ordering of the same basic elements. In this way one can never get beyond the domain of one's own past experiences.

This leads to "disastrous consequences". Assertions about other minds in the ordinary sense cannot even be formulated in the constitution-system. For these assertions likewise cannot have any other content than relations between my own experiences; everything else is nothing but scientifically undescribable imagination. Statements about other minds are equivalent to statements about the bodily expressive symptoms of unowned mental states which, on the physical level, are constituted out of the stream of my experiences. And for analogous reasons, statements about the future turn into statements about the past. For the concept of the future likewise is a logical construction out of experience, and does not refer to something originally given in experience. Likewise, inductive generalizations from the past to the future are thus deprived of any foundation. "Thus the very end of philosophy has, indeed, been reached" (p. 53).

This penetrating critique is, however, accompanied by the highest compliment: "Even this mere sketch of the constitution-system represents an eminent achievement, admirable and characterized by unsurpassed abstract acuteness and beautiful logical neatness" (p. 29).

In his reply (loc. cit.) Carnap concedes that all material-psychological questions are still open for debate, including the question whether experiences are indivisible units or exhibit a certain original, internal multiplicity, and consequently also the question whether, and on what level, quasi-analysis is applicable. He further admits that it is an open question whether there is a difference between real and ideal order, since this depends again on the question of internal multiplicity of the given.

Carnap's "Der Logische Aufbau der Welt" has been subjected to clearly formulated and fundamental criticism also by Weinberg,[106] a criticism likewise devoted to the demonstration of "disastrous consequences": the belief in a physical world existing independently of one's own experience cannot be justified, statements about other minds are meaningless, and communication (and thus intersubjectivity) is impossible. If the only meaningful assertions are assertions about my own experiences, then statements about inferred physical objects as well as statements about experiences of other people cannot be meaningful. The latter must be replaced by assertions about the forms of outward behavior of other people. The former are logically equivalent to the latter and it is therefore logically permissible to substitute one for the other. If nevertheless, in making such statements, one thinks of unowned experiences of the same kind as one's own, such thoughts will have to be dismissed as irrelevant associated imagery. And therefore one can react to the statement made by other people only as to behavioral facts, not as to symbols (p. 219). It is alleged to follow that communication is altogether impossible, and that accordingly there is no such thing as intersubjectivity (p. 222).

In judging Carnap's "Logischer Aufbau" one ought not to forget that what the whole constitution-system is exclusively about is definitions of concepts. Carnap says explicitly in the preface (p. II, III): "What is here in question is the reducibility of one item of knowledge to others", and "that the answer to the question of reducibility leads to a unified, as it were genealogical reduction-system of the concepts used in science, which requires but a small number of primitive concepts".

The definitions should ultimately be framed exclusively in terms of relations between the experiences belonging to a definite ("my") stream of experience—this, after all, is the purpose of the whole constitution-system. The conceptual entities thus constituted are nothing but forms of order among these experiences and their designations are only abbreviations for them. Whether they designate moreover something existing in itself, "is a metaphysical question which is out of place in science" (p. 220).

Nevertheless, Carnap's constitution-system has not by any means made it clear whether all scientific concepts, or which scientific concepts, can be constituted by a mere re-arranging of experiences. For a rigorous constitution was carried out only for the solipsistic concepts. That the latter can be constructed on the sole basis of private experiences is beyond doubt anyway. The constitution, however, has only been *sketched* for the higher levels of concept-formation, and a cogent proof of the reducibility of these levels to relations between experiences is, therefore, still outstanding.

Carnap's constitution-system is intended to satisfy two requirements: it is supposed to amount to a rational reconstruction of concept-formation such as actually occurs in science, and by means of which the world is logically constructed, and it is supposed to accomplish this purpose on the basis of relations between experiences alone. In order to satisfy this latter requirement, he makes use of the concept of logical equivalence. Two propositional functions are logically equivalent if they always lead to propositions of identical truth-value, i.e. propositions which are either both true or both false. All that matters is their truth-value, while their meanings may be vastly different. From this point of view, however, concepts are definable in terms of relations between experiences only if these definitions are logically equivalent to the other methods of definition. This seems to be possible since conceptual contents must somehow be connected with experience if they are to give rise to decidable assertions about the world. These experiential criteria may, therefore, well be employed for the definitional determination of concepts. It is clear, however, that in this manner concepts can be constituted only insofar as they express no more than re-arrangements of experiences. Any *other* kind of meaning to which these definitions might be equivalent is incapable of constitution in this manner; it degenerates into mere "associative imagery'" which is logically irrelevant and need not be attended to in logical analysis. But the concepts of other consciousness and of the future and of the unconscious prove that there are concepts with this other kind of meaning which are likewise involved in the constitution of the world. Concepts of objects "which are not given in experience" (p. 180) can be constituted only insofar as they merely express re-arrangements of quasi-elements of experiences. Any other kind of meaning is necessarily lost in Carnap's constitution-system. This circumstance is not due to the choice of a solipsistic basis. Even if *several* streams of experience were chosen as bases, concepts of extra-mental entities could not be defined, although the concept of other consciousness would be definable.

If the entire constitution-system involves only concept-formation, in other words, definitions, then there is no room in it for existential assertions. This leads to the following consequence: It is clear that attributions of sense-qualities to unobserved world-points transcend the frame of a constitutional definition. But the assertion "that an analogous part of the thing *exists* in the unobserved part of space" (p. 180) is an existence-assertion, and consequently of altogether different order than definitions. It is an extrapolation, not a mere "re-arrangement of primitive data" (p. 176) which is what such constitutions of concepts are. Whether the defined object exists always requires separate proof. But such a proof would be out of place here, since the constitution of concepts is not concerned with this question of existence. There is no question of reality here. The same holds for the attribution of *unconscious* states which are constituted on the basis of conscious states as "generic components of experiences" (quality-classes, components of qualities, or complexes of such), and which are attributed to time-points in particular (not just to world-points), analogously to unseen color-points. This procedure does not even enable constitution of the *concept* of the unconscious, and at any rate it cannot be used to *supplement* my consciousness for the purpose of establishing within the total domain of solipsistic data a more complete, though not absolutely complete, order of laws than within the partial domain of my conscious experiences.

It is, for analogous reasons, beyond doubt that the concept of other consciousness cannot be anything else than a concept representing a mere "re-ordering of my experiences"[107] (p. 193), but that this is so only as long as what is involved is constitutional definition, and not an existence assertion.

What is true of the various levels of constitution also

holds for the intersubjective world: all "these constitutions consist, not in a hypothetical inference or fictitious postulation of something which is not given, but in a re-arrangement of the given" (p. 200). Inferences beyond my experiences contradict the requirement of mere re-arrangement and are therefore prohibited.

It is not the task of a constitution-system of concepts to make *statements* about the world at all, neither about other minds nor about the future, but only to construct *concepts*. But since all concepts in Carnap's system represent only re-arrangements of quasi-elements of the stream of one's own experiences, it follows that one cannot make *statements* in the ordinary sense with these concepts unsupplemented by others. Carnap's theory of constitution, nevertheless, has the merit, which ought not to be underestimated, of exhibiting clearly the implications and limitations of a constitution of concepts on a purely experiential-immanent basis.

Carnap's book was the exclusive, or at least the primary, focus of attention in historical reports about the philosophy of the Vienna Circle. Those numerous publications which later issued from the Vienna Circle have been hardly taken notice of. Yet, the doctrine of the "Aufbau" has already been in part superseded. Carnap himself is responsible for a fundamental correction, in the essay, significant in several respects, "Testability and Meaning".[108]

There are concepts, like "visible" or "soluble", concepts of dispositional properties, which it is difficult to define in the manner of the constitution-system. A property of this kind consists in a disposition to a kind of reaction under specified conditions. A dispositional property, therefore, is not directly observable—you cannot see

the solubility of a substance by looking at it—, though
it is discoverable in no other way than by observations. A substance is soluble if it dissolves when it is immersed in a suitable liquid. The concept of a dispositional property is reducible to experiences by means of
a conditional sentence of the indicated sort, an implication which specifies under what conditions the dispositional property in question is present, and a second implication which specifies under what conditions it is ab-
sent; both implications may under circumstances be combined into one single implication.

But this method does not amount to definition. Such
a pair of reduction-sentences, or a bilateral reduction-sentence, determines the concept of the dispositional property only for those situations in which the test-condition,
mentioned by the implication, is fulfilled. In those cases,
however, where the condition is not realised, neither the
presence nor the absence of the dispositional property
in question can be asserted. If a given object has never
been immersed in the corresponding liquid, the question
of whether it is soluble in the liquid or not cannot be
decided. One will have to look, in that case, for further
test-conditions expressed by new implications, in order
that the concept be determined for those conditions also
and a decision become possible. For this purpose one
might, e.g., set up the implication that if one of two
samples of the same substance has proved to be soluble,
then the other is likewise to be regarded as soluble even
though it has never satisfied the respective condition.
But in this manner the domain of indeterminacy can be
only narrowed, not completely eliminated. Theoretically
it always remains possible to raise the question whether
these implications hold also for those kinds of situations

in which they have not been tested. A definition, on the contrary, determines a concept once and for all, for all possible situations. If reduction sentences, therefore, were employed as definitions, they would be laid down as valid beyond the domain of application for which they were originally formulated. These implications are frequently empirically discovered laws of nature, and hence it may happen that they prove inapplicable to new kinds of situations. Interpreted as a definition, such a statement would in that eventuality have to be abandoned; but interpreted as a mere reduction-sentence which claims to apply only to a limited empirically ascertained domain, it would remain valid and only call for supplementation by new reduction-sentences. A definition may be formed out of the reduction-sentences, the implications, only when the conditions of reaction are determined for *all* cases. In general, however, the incompleteness of the test-conditions makes it impossible to replace a concept introduced, like the disposition concepts, by reduction-sentences, with primitive concepts and thus to eliminate it. Thus we have to acknowledge concepts which are, indeed, reducible to relations between experiences, but are not definable in terms of the latter.

This entails a correction of the original conception which is of fundamental importance. Carnap's constitution-system was dominated by the positivist-empiricist principle that every empirical concept of science is reducible to, and accordingly definable by, concepts expressing relations between experiences. After all, the exhibition of such a reduction was the very purpose of the constitution-system. This thesis is now subjected to a basic restriction. Reducibility is still maintained, but unqualified definability and thereby replaceability by relations of experiences cannot be claimed any more.

Kaila, however, made an attempt to reinstate without restrictions the thesis of definability.[109] An implication, an if-then relationship, which serves to reduce a dispositional property to observables, is not suited for the definition of such a property because it becomes useless in case the response-condition it specifies is not fulfilled at all. Kaila therefore adds the requirement that the antecedent of such if-then relations must not be vacuous, that predications of such a property should always be based on actual observations. This, nevertheless, is not satisfactory as a complete solution of the difficulties. For the fact still remains that in most cases a complete set of reduction-sentences is unobtainable, and this difficulty is not overcome by Kaila's amendment.

The concepts of thing-properties and of physical state-variables are of the same sort as the disposition concepts. The statement "at time t there is at place O the thing D" cannot be replaced by a conditional statement about relations of experiences of the kind "anybody who at time t were placed at O would have such and such percepts". For an enumeration of such percepts would have to include not only visual percepts from all possible perspectives and all possible tactual percepts of the thing, but also percepts arising from indirect observations, such as photography etc. Even if the number of such possible percepts should not be infinite, it would still be impossible to describe them exhaustively by a huge conjunction, since one cannot a priori foresee all possibilities of perception. The same holds, e.g., with regard to the intensity of an electrical current. It can be determined in terms of the deflection of a magnetic needle or in terms of the heating of a conductor or in terms of the amount of hydrogen given off by the water through which the current passes, and by means of many more tests. Any one of these methods of measurement is describable in terms of an indefinite number of possible perceptions, and it is evidently impossible to describe these possibilities exhaustively by means of implications of the form "if such and such conditions, then such and such perceptions". It is an indefinite, open conjunction of such implications which is equivalent to the concept of such a property. Hence it is impossible to define these property-concepts in terms of perceptions, relations between experiences, i.e. to replace and eliminate them by concepts referring to the latter. It follows that not all concepts are definable in this manner, and consequently the introduction of concepts by reduction-sentences is unavoidable.

Accordingly we must distinguish, in any language, three kinds of signs: (1) primitive signs, introduced without the help of other signs, (2) indirectly introduced signs, subdivided into signs indirectly introduced (a) by definitions, (b) by reduction-sentences. It is not, however, just a small and insignificant group of concepts which require to be introduced by reduction-sentences, but rather a group of concepts which are indispensable for science. Thus a state of affairs of far-reaching significance has been uncovered, whose implications have not yet been sufficiently examined.

II. THE VERIFICATION-BASIS OF EMPIRICAL STATEMENTS

1. *Verifying Statements*

Just as the Vienna Circle faced the clarification of the content of empirical concepts through their reduction to data of experience as a fundamental task of empiricism, so they took upon themselves the further task of clarifying the content and validity of empirical *propositions* through their reduction to elementary propositions. Here again Wittgenstein's "Tractatus" served as the starting-point suggesting, at first, the general line of approach. Wittgenstein borrowed from Russell's "Principia Mathematica" the fundamental division of propositions into compound and simple ones, "molecular" and "atomic" propositions. Atomic propositions are defined negatively as singular propositions which do not themselves contain propositions as components, where a singular proposition is any proposition which does not contain the concepts "all" or "some". Molecular propositions are likewise singular, but they contain one or two or more atomic propositions. Such compound propositions have the form of conjunctions or disjunctions or implications or negations. Negative propositions also count as compound since they contain the proposition which is negated.

Wittgenstein, now, emphasized the new, important insight that the truth-value of compound propositions depends exclusively on the truth-values of the simple propositions which are their components; the former are "truth-functions" of the latter. Consequently, what alone matters is the truth-value of the simple, atomic propositions from which the truth-values of the compound propositions are derivable by pure logic.

The truth-conditions for propositions of the simplest form can be given directly: they are true if the object designated by the proper name has in fact the property or relation designated by the predicate. For the other forms of propositions, those containing component propositions, the truth-conditions are determined indirectly. Wittgenstein showed how the truth-value of conjunctions, disjunctions, implications and negations depends upon the truth-values of the component propositions, by virtue of the meanings of "and", "or", "if-then", "not", the "logical constants". When two propositions are combined, there are many combinatorial possibilities of their truth-values, altogether 2^n possibilities for propositions with n components. It can easily be seen that a conjunction of two propositions is true if and only if both component propositions are true; if, on the other hand, one or both component propositions are false, the conjunction itself is false. On the other hand, a disjunction involving the inclusive "or", distinguished from the exclusive "either-or", is false only if both component propositions are false. Similarly, an implication is true in three cases and false if the first component proposition, the antecedent, is true and the second, the consequent, is false. A negation is true if the negated proposition is false, and false if the negated proposition is true. But one could conversely define these forms of propositional connection in terms of the form of truth-dependence, by indicating what combinations of truth-values of the component propositions yield true propositions of the given form and what combinations yield false propositions of the given form. Thus the disjunction of propositions p and q is determined by the circumstance that it is true if both, or exactly one, proposition is true, and false only if both are false. In that case the *meanings* of these connectives need not be considered at all. The logical constants, then, may be determined in two ways: either on the basis of their meanings, like words, or in terms of the truth-con-

ditions of the compound propositions formed by means
of them.

The truth of a *universal* proposition is a function of
the truth of all those singular propositions which fall
under the universal proposition and which are determined by a direct truth-condition. Therefore a universal
proposition must be capable of being formulated as a
conjunction of singular propositions.[110]

The next and most important task, therefore, consisted in finding the atomic propositions and to determine
them on the basis of their logical form. Wittgenstein
identified them with the propositions he called "elementary propositions".[111] They are propositions which can
be *immediately* compared with reality, i.e. with the data
of experience. Such propositions must exist, for otherwise language would be unrelated to reality. All propositions which are not themselves elementary propositions
are necessarily truth-functions of elementary propositions.
Hence all empirical propositions must be reducible to
propositions about the given, they must be translatable
into such propositions, unless they are themselves of the
latter kind. If a sentence does not admit of such reduction it must be declared as meaningless, since one does
not know, in that case, what it is all about. The reduction is made possible by a family-tree of concepts which
exhibits their reducibility to relations between experiences, the sort of reduction sketched in Carnap's constitution-system. In this way the empiricist theories of meaning, concepts and propositions are all interconnected.

In consideration of the fact that atomic or elementary
propositions are assertions about experiences, it was assumed by the Vienna Circle that they are to be found

among the so-called "protocol sentences".[112] Protocol sentences are supposed to describe the simplest knowable states of affairs, and not to contain any sentences obtained by interpretation of the given. They are supposed, therefore, to designate the immediately given. But as to just what sentences satisfy these requirements there was no clarity. These sentences were regarded as being about the given, but for traditional positivism the "given" consisted in sense- and feeling- qualities, for Carnap it consisted in total experiences and relations between them, while Neurath considered physical situations as the starting-point. What thus remained uncertain was just the foundations of empirical knowledge. What they had primarily in mind were experiential, preferably perceptual protocols. In place of the original subjective form with "I" and "now" and "here" Neurath insisted on an objective form for protocol-sentences, containing the name of the observer, descriptions of time and place, and the concept of perception. For example, "N perceived at time t and at place O such and such". Good examples can be found among the protocols used in psychological experiments. Although no such protocol sentences are formulated for physical or biological experiments, one knows nonetheless that such protocol sentences can be reconstructed as their ultimate foundations. "If an investigator, e.g., writes down 'under such and such circumstances the pointer indicates 10.5', he knows that this means 'two black marks coincide' and that the words 'under such and such circumstances . . . ' must similarly be resolved into definite protocol sentences".[113]

At first the protocol sentences (perceptual judgments) were regarded as absolutely certain. They are "sentences which themselves do not require confirmation, but serve

118

as basis for all other scientific sentences".[114] Neurath disputed this claim of absolute certainty;[115] according to him, protocol sentences too might under circumstances be declared invalid.[116] For they are never without interpretative content, they are no more primitive than other empirical sentences, they are just as hypothetical and thus corrigible. It is altogether impossible to compare statements with the given, with experience, with something extra-linguistic; statements can be compared only with statements. Carnap joined Neurath in this contention. Protocol sentences enjoy no privilege over other kinds of sentences.[117] Certain concrete sentences are adopted as protocol sentences, i.e. as terminal points of the process of reduction. "There are no absolutely basic sentences in the construction of science".[118] It is a matter of decision, of convention, where one wishes to make a halt. Such was the incisive turn in the conception of protocol sentences, a turn which meant again the elimination of a last remnant of absolutism from epistemology.

But thus a new big question had to be confronted. If protocol-sentences cease to be absolutely certain and become corrigible, how is one going to determine under what conditions a protocol sentence must be abandoned and under what conditions it must be retained? The criterion proposed by Neurath was mutual coherence of empirical sentences. This criterion, however, leaves the door open to arbitrary decisions. If a given protocol sentence is consistent with the system of hitherto accepted sentences, one may either "cancel" it or instead accept it "and modify the system in such a way that this sentence may without inconsistency be incorporated into it".[119] In this manner, though, any system of sentences whatever may be maintained by simply cancelling incompatible protocol sentences. The Michelson-Morley experiment, in that case, would not have necessitated the construction of a new theory, the theory of relativity. If one leaves it a matter of arbitrary decision whether an incompatible protocol sentence is or is not valid, one falls a prey to conventionalism and abandons empiricism.

At this point Schlick entered the controversy with his essay "Ueber das Fundament der Erkenntnis".[120] Mutual agreement of empirical sentences means consistency; but the latter suffices only if we are dealing with a purely conceptual system like mathematics; for the knowledge of *facts* mere consistency is not sufficient, what is needed is consistency with definite sentences which cannot be freely chosen since they are characterized by incorrigibility. These incorrigible sentences consist in assertions about one's own present perceptions. But they are not the protocol sentences which stand at the *beginning* of knowledge; they represent, indeed, the origin of knowledge, but not its logical basis. Those privileged sentences are rather those that constitute the *end-point of knowledge*. They are those observational reports which yield verification (or falsification).

Verification occurs when the correspondence of a predicted state of affairs with the observed state of affairs is ascertained. An observable consequence is deduced from the hypothesis to be verified, which is then compared with the actually observed state of affairs. E.g., an astronomical calculation yields the result that at such and such a time a star should be observable through a telescope directed in such and such a way. The verifying observation, then, might be formulated by the report "there coincides here-now a bright and a dark point (the star and the point of intersection of a pair of cross-hairs)".

Such an observation-report always has the form "here now such and such", where "such and such" designates something immediately given, not the latter's objective interpretation, e.g. "there occurs a pain here-now" or "black is adjacent to white here-now". What is characteristic of these observation-sentences is that indicator-terms like "now", "here", "this" belong essentially to their logical form. No definite content is designated by these words, they simply refer to something immediately and presently given. The meaning of such a sentence can be understood only by following this reference and attending to what is referred to. Consequently, to understand such a sentence and to verify it is all one, for that which constitutes its meaning is, after all, immediately given. While normally understanding the meaning of a sentence and ascertaining its truth are two totally distinct phases of the process of verification, they here coincide. In grasping the meaning of such an assertion, which Schlick calls a "Konstatierung", one simultaneously recognizes its truth. Usually this is so only for analytic sentences. With regard to them too, verification coincides with interpretation, since their truth is knowable by analysis of the sentence alone. In the case of synthetic sentences, on the contrary, understanding their meaning does not involve knowledge of their truth or falsity. The latter question, the question of truth or falsity, can be decided only by experience, confrontation with observation-sentences. Since in understanding a sense-statement one implicitly verifies it, such a statement is absolutely true and certain, just like an analytic statement. It is final and irrevocable, and constitutes for this reason the basis of empirical knowledge.[121]

But no matter how acutely and persuasively this conception of sense-statements may be developed, it still does not amount to a definitive solution. The whole conception suffers from a serious defect. Sense-statements are absolutely valid only insofar as they are assertions about experience at the present moment. They cannot be used as permanent assertions. For in that case they become falsified by the occurrence of the words "here", "now", "this" which always refer to the present moment. But they cannot be formulated as protocol sentences either, like "NN perceived at time t and at place O such and such", since such a formulation deprives them of their absolute validity and turns them into hypotheses. A sense-statement is completely different from a protocol sentence. This is evident from the circumstance that every protocol sentence contains implicitly a sense-statement. For the above protocol sentence could be alternatively formulated thus "NN verified at time t and at place O such and such a sense-statement". The whole sentence cannot be synonymous with a sentence contained in it. Immediate perceptions form the occasion for the formulation of protocol sentences, but they themselves cannot be protocoled. Being of the nature of monologues, they lack intersubjectivity. And they have but momentary validity, for which reason they are useless as basic premises on which to build. They can function only as endpoints of the process of verification. This would not diminish their value if it were not for the fact that incorrigible sense-statements are assertions which it is even impossible to keep fixed, as they are but momentary assertions. "A genuinely immediate perception cannot be verbally expressed. For, the moment I write down the indicator-term 'here', 'now', they change their meanings".[122] Assertions of this kind have no place in a system of propositions. All they can do is to form the occasion for the formulation of other assertions which, however, are only hypothetical protocol sentences.

Schlick's concept of "Konstatierung" was at once subjected to criticism in the Vienna Circle. First Neurath criticised[123] the concept, its lack of clarity, the supposition of absolute validity, and the involved concept of correspondence to reality. Then again Popper raised weighty objections and expressed a new point of view, in his significant book "Die Logik der Forschung", 1935,[124] which exercised a decisive influence on the conceptual development of the Vienna Circle. Popper replaced the fundamental conception expressed by Wittgenstein's doctrine of elementary propositions and by the Vienna Circle's doctrine of protocol sentences, by an altogether different conception. The edifice of scientific knowledge should not be erected upon singular propositions about experiences, nor should it be reduced to the latter as expressing its proper content.

For every scientific proposition goes far beyond what is known on the basis of immediate experience, being formulated in terms of general concepts, universals. The latter cannot be reduced to classes of experiences, they are indefinable in terms of particulars and determined only by linguistic usage. Popper, indeed, denies on principle that there are concepts admitting of constitution, i.e. empirically definable concepts; in other words, he rejects the theory of constitution, though without detailed argumentation. It is therefore impossible, according to Popper, to make an assertion which would actually express a definite datum of experience as unique and particular. This is why perceptual judgments cannot claim any privileged position. Accordingly all assertions what-

ever are hypotheses. Any attempt, such as Schlick's, to
found science upon assertions carrying the quality of
absolute conviction, appears to him therefore as psychologism and thus as doomed to futility from the start.
Feelings of absolute conviction, like the feeling of self-
evidence, are purely psychological matters, as indeed
Schlick himself emphasized. He described the characteristic feature of a "Konstatierung'" as "a feeling of fulfilment" of our expectation and wrote "that incorrigible
sense-statements (Konstatierungen) or observation-sentences fulfill their true mission as soon as we experience
this peculiar feeling of satisfaction".[125] Schlick's incorrigible sense-statements express, to this extent, rather
mere experiences than judgments, something psychological rather than something logical. Perceptions, experiences funish, indeed, knowledge of facts, but only in the
psychological, genetic sense; they cannot be regarded as
grounds of the validity of factual knowledge. The truth
of assertions cannot be guaranteed by experiences, for
scientific assertions are intersubjective and hence can be
validated only in terms of intersubjective foundations,
not in terms of subjective experiences.

Any assertion says more than what is actually given
in a verifying experience. For verification, after all,
always involves that an experience occurs *under definite
circumstances*. It is only a luminous point in such and
such a neighborhood at a definite time which verifies the
passage of a star through a pair of cross-hairs and represents a valid astronomical observation. Whether these
circumstances obtain must again be testable, and thus
a given statement implies a plurality of further statements.[126] The validity of a statement, then, is tested by
deducing from it, in conjunction with statements already

124

established as valid, consequences which are testable with comparative ease. Such consequences must consist in singular propositions which assert that such and such exists at a definite space-time position, i.e. singular existence assertions. Whether what they assert is actually the case must admit of intersubjective test in terms of observations; the object or event in question must therefore be observable. "Observability", in contradistinction to "observation", is not a psychological but an epistemological concept; it is introduced by Popper as an indefinable primitive concept. It is in this manner that Popper establishes the contact between empirical knowledge and perceptual experience. He calls such sentences about observable events "basic sentences". Not that they are identical with what was meant by "protocol sentences". The latter are sentences about actual perceptions, about facts of experience. Popper's "basic sentences", however, assert nothing about what has actually been experienced. Nor are they sentences which have already been accepted; they are but statements of *conceivable* facts which follow from a given hypothesis. Whether they correspond to the facts, whether they are true or false, is still a question to be decided. *Conceivable,* logically possible, basic sentences constitute the material in terms of which hypotheses are tested, and those among them which have been *accepted* constitute the basis for the confirmation or disconfirmation of the tested hypotheses. One single basic sentence, however, describing an unrepeatable event, cannot confirm or disconfirm a hypothesis. For in order to be testable, an event must be intersubjectively repeatable. And the assertion of the occurrence of such a repeatable event is already a hypothesis of the lowest order of generality. To this extent, then, the assertions on which the validity of empirical knowledge is founded are one step removed from descriptions of experiences.

Insofar as protocol sentences are about perceptions they are not easily testable. It is notorious that statements about particular perceptions are more difficult to test than, say, statements about things or processes in the external world. It is for this reason that the basic sentences in terms of which decisions of acceptance or rejection of a hypothesis are made are as a rule sentences of this kind and not protocol sentences.

Since basic sentences are not absolutely certain but hypothetical only, they are themselves subject to test. Such tests must in turn be applicable to the sentences in terms of which they are tested, and so on ad infinitum. But this infinite regress does not amount to a *reductio ad absurdum* of this theory, since it is not actual testing, but only testability of each sentence serving as a test-sentence which is necessary. It is possible and necessary to stop after a sentence which appears sufficiently confirmed has been reached, and to break the test-procedure off. There are no absolutely ultimate sentences, elementary sentences, sentences which need not be tested any more as they are absolutely certain and incorrigible. If we acknowledge certain basic sentences as decisive, this is only because they are the sentences about which intersubjective agreement is most readily obtainable, the sentences most easily verified. This means that the sentences constituting the ulimate test-basis are selected by convention. They are valid by convention only.

As decisive basic sentences those sentences are selected which assert something intersubjectively observable and are thus reducible to experience. But experiences do not constitute the logical grounds of their validity. Experiences only *motivate* their acceptance or stipulation. It must be said, though, that Popper does not enter into a detailed discussion of the question how basic sentences are related to experiences; he confines himself to the general formula "that the decision to accept a given basic sentence is connected with experiences" (ibid., p. 62). In admitting this connection, Popper accepts at least a trace of empiricism.[127] But he himself confesses that the theory he defends resembles conventionalism. For inasmuch as the decisive basic sentences are accepted by convention, the validity of an hypothesis rests ultimately on conventions made for reasons of expediency. "Basic sentences are accepted by decision, by convention, they are stipulations. Limits are imposed upon possible decisions by the fact that we cannot accept individual basic sentences in logical isolation but only in the context of testing a *theory*" (op. cit., p. 62). A theory is not elected as valid "through logical reduction to experience; we prefer that theory which excels in the contest consisting in the selection of theories, the theory which is most rigorously testable and which has most successfully survived the rigorous tests so far made" (op. cit., p. 64). What distinguishes Popper's conception from conventionalism is the circumstance that according to the former it is not the most general propositions but the basic sentences which are conventions. Popper's conception differs from positivism as well as from empiricism in that experience is not the *ground of validity* of basic sentences, but that the acceptance of a basic sentence consists, from the logical point of view, in nothing but an arbitrary convention, a decision which is but psychologically determined by experience. (ibid., p. 65).

127

Nevertheless empiricism may still be maintained if we consider that all that is determined by arbitrary conventions is which basic sentences should be chosen to break the process of testing off. The question, however, which basic sentences should be acknowledged as decisive, is answered on the basis of observation-sentences. They are regarded as valid because they agree with all relevant observation-reports. Verifying statements must either be themselves observation-reports or be ultimately reducible to such. And they are accepted as valid just as long as no reason for doubting them presents itself. The latter happens whenever they get into contradiction with accepted sentences. In that case either the former or the latter are re-examined, both in the same way. But what leads to the final decision is always agreement (or conflict) with observation-reports which themselves are consistent not only with the basic sentences to be verified but also with the corresponding reports of other observers. If we look at the situation in this way, we still come to the conclusion that it is observation-reports and not arbitrary conventions which constitute the ground of validity of empirical assertions. To be sure, a conventional component is still involved inasmuch as it depends on our decision whether we consider a given basic sentence as sufficiently reliable or as still in need of further confirmation. But what is thus decided upon is only whether the sentence should be further tested; the result of such a test, however, or even the accepted validity of the sentence without further test, is not determined by convention but by observation-reports.[128] What is a convention is only the decision to desist from further confirmation, not the *objects* selected as verifying sentences. Rather the latter are determined by their relations to observation-reports.

The theories which prove the most successful are just those which are in best agreement with intersubjectively consistent observation-reports.

The crux of the whole problem of protocol sentences is that language must refer to something extra-linguistic, not just because without such reference language would be devoid of meaning, but because otherwise a system of sentences could not be characterized as a system of empirical knowledge. It is this idea which motivated Schlick. If it were possible to remain entirely within a language, the process of verification would be purely logical or formal. But the concept of verification cannot be adequately analyzed in terms of syntactic concepts alone. This has been demonstrated by Carnap's endeavors. If we stick to purely formal analysis, we cannot mark out valid empirical sentences as against invalid ones, since the validity of empirical sentences cannot be determined on the basis of their logical form.[129] Neurath tried to overcome this difficulty with the help of the coherence theory. But in this way no uniqueness can be achieved; one falls a prey to arbitrariness and abandons empiricism. The purely syntactic approach to linguistic analysis makes the problem of verification insoluble since this approach ignores relations to anything extra-linguistic. The semantic point of view alone provides a basis for such relations. But the problem of the relation of verifying sentences to perceptual experience has not yet been completely solved in the Vienna Circle; on the contrary, the acceptance of physicalism has even complicated the problem.[130]

The conception of observation-reports as epistemologically basic must be abandoned if it takes the form in which it was maintained by traditional empiricism and which was combated by Popper as "inductivism". Ac-

cording to this conception observation-reports are logically primary and all empirical knowledge, including the
knowledge of universal propositions, results from an inductive ordering and integration of these reports. But
induction is justifiable as a cogent logical procedure only
if a major premise of supreme generality, a principle of
induction, is supplied for the logical deduction of universal propositions from particular propositions. Such a
principle would have to be a universal synthetic proposition about reality, about the uniformity of Nature. It
obviously cannot in turn be inductively justified, since
this would amount to a petitio principii. Nor can it be
introduced axiomatically, since in that case it would be
refuted the very first time a generalization is subsequently
disconfirmed.[131] It was one of the earliest and most fundamental insights of the Vienna Circle that no deductive
or logical justification of induction is at all possible.
Even though Schlick says that scientific laws originate
from observation-sentences "gradually through that process which is called 'induction' and which consists in
nothing else than the fact that, stimulated by protocol-
sentences, I formulate tentatively universal sentences
('hypotheses') from which those former sentences . . . are
logically deducible", he is nevertheless entirely clear
about the non-logical, merely psychological character of
this process: "Induction is nothing but methodologically
regulated guesswork, a psychological, biological process
whose discussion certainly has nothing to do with
logic".[132] The *validity* of empirical statements is not
based on induction but on the subsequent verification
of tentatively formulated hypotheses. If sentences which
follow from the latter "are synonymous with later observation-sentences, then the hypotheses are considered as

confirmed until such time as observation-sentences appear which are inconsistent with the sentences deduced from the hypotheses" (ibid.). As regards "inductivism" and "deductivism", there was unanimity between Popper and the Vienna Circle.

Once again we are here confronted with a fundamental reform of empiricism. From the standpoint of rigorous logic, the traditional founding of empiricism upon induction must be surrendered. The conception of empirical knowledge which J. St. Mill and Mach and even Wittgenstein adhered to, viz. that empirical knowledge is based upon singular observation-sentences which are certain in themselves and whose integration leads to natural laws, has become untenable. Far from having given, in this fashion, even an accurate psychological description of the origin of empirical knowledge, one certainly cannot thus logically reconstruct it.[133] All empirical knowledge consists in the formulation of hypotheses which always *go beyond* the given, always assert more than the latter, even if they are singular statements. Hypotheses are not verified once and for all by observations antecedent to their formulation, but they always have to be confirmed by subsequent tests. Their verification depends upon correspondence with intersubjectively acceptable observation-reports. Owing to the permanent possibility of further confirmation, no empirical assertions can claim final validity, but only provisional, corrigible validity. And the fact that thus intersubjective observability is recognized as a necessary condition does not imply that empirical validity has been reduced to conventions. After all, it is not a matter of arbitrary convention whether we accept these observation-sentences and reject those; rather verification is determined by an intersubjectively ascertainable regularity of experiences. It is thus that validity is determined "on the basis of experience", in contrast to the inductive conception.

2. Verification of Universal Statements

The validity of *universal* propositions constitutes a difficult problem even for a non-inductivist conception. Wittgenstein tried, in keeping with his discovery of truth-functionality, to represent the truth of universal propositions as a function of the truth of singular propositions. This requires that universal propositions be analyzable into conjunctions of singular propositions, which in most cases is not possible. There are two kinds of generality: "all" might signify a definite finite collection considered as one, a definite class whose elements can be enumerated, e.g. all the inhabitants of Vienna as they are counted in a population census. But "all" may also signify a class which is defined only in terms of definite properties (predicates or relations) and is for this reason an indefinite, not closed but open aggregate and whose elements, consequently, do not admit of complete enumeration. This is the kind of generality which is involved in laws of nature. It follows that only universal propositions of the first kind can be transformed into conjunctions and established as true on the basis of the truth of the conjuncts. This procedure is inapplicable to universal propositions of the second kind. Accordingly Wittgenstein, and his followers Ramsey[134] and Schlick[135], admitted only atomic propositions and molecular propositions composed of such as genuine propositions with cognitive content; for they alone were assumed to be capable of conclusive verification, in contrast to propositions of unrestricted generality. The implications of this view are far-reaching. It leads not only to the elimination of the actual infinite from mathematics—a position which Felix Kaufmann attempted to justify—[136] but furthermore implies that the *laws of nature* cannot be interpreted, as they ordinarily are, as propositions of *unrestricted generality*. If, on the other hand, laws of nature are interpreted as *molecular propositions,* i.e. as mere syntheses of singular propositions in the form of conjunctions, and as truth-functions of the latter, then they would contain nothing but *established statements of fact* and there would be no such thing as *predictions* for new cases. Hence Schlick regarded universal sentences expressing natural laws as only rules or formulae for the formulation of genuine assertions,[137] i.e., of the specific assertions which are deducible from a universal proposition (a law of nature), as for example, "under such and such conditions the pointer of a definite measuring instrument will coincide with a definite scale-mark". According to this view, the laws of nature, and thus the theoretical structure of the exact sciences which is the foundation of the technical arts, would have no cognitive content at all; the laws of nature would assert nothing about the empirical world, being nothing else but a species of syntactic rules.[138] A law of nature, accordingly, is only a sentence-schema, a "sentential function", and obviously such an expression could not be regarded as a factual assertion. It contains nothing but a methodological rule. The schema serves to enable the formation of definite assertions by substitution of concrete data for its variables. It is only the latter that are verifiable, while verification is, of course, meaningless with respect to the sentential schema itself. The outlined theory of meaning has been criticized by Kaila[139] who argued that the meaningfulness of a universal statement does not require its *conclusive* verifiability. The significance of a statement is, according to Kaila, independent of its verifiability; it presupposes only that the meanings of the constituent expressions be known and that the statement be syntactically well formed. It is the singular statements which are deducible from a universal statement that have to be verifiable, not their total conjunction. Universal statements derive their cognitive importance just from the impossibility of complete verification, since they make assertions about future cases only if they are not completely verifiable; which would not be the case if their content were exhausted by a finite number of cases.

Carnap's analysis of language has made it clear that it is not necessary to exclude unrestrictedly universal statements, that such a prohibition is nothing but a stipulation which one may or may not see fit to make. It is a stipulation concerning the formation-rules of a language, and to which there are alternatives that may be freely chosen. Carnap sketches an entire ladder of languages, by admitting or excluding on the various levels of the hierarchy sentences of this or that form.[140]

Sentences of the simplest form, atomic or elementary sentences, are singular sentences containing a "primitive" predicate. By the latter is meant an observable predicate, or a predicate introduced by an atomic chain of reduction-sentences. These sentences are contrasted with compound sentences. Within the latter class, a fundamental distinction must be observed in accordance with the kind of operations by which the sentences are formed. The operations of sentential connection (conjunction, implication etc.) lead to *molecular* sentences, the operations of universal and existential quantification to *generalised* sentences. If the quantifiers are restricted to finite domains, the latter sentences are transformable into conjunctions or disjunctions, and so into molecular sentences. It is the sentences of *unrestricted* generality which are controversial. These sentences are in turn divisible into different types, accordingly as they contain universal or existential operators or both, and in accordance with the number of such operators. Thus we obtain an indefinite series of languages of increasing complexity.

The simplest language is the one in which only sentences of restricted generality, molecular sentences, can be formed. In the next higher, i.e. richer form of language unrestrictedly universal sentences of the simplest kind, viz. those with one single universal operator, are admissible. Next follows the language in which also existential sentences of the simplest kind, viz. those with one single existential operator, are admitted. Then again comes the language in which unrestrictedly universal sentences with an existential operator are introduced. The higher forms of languages result through alternating additions of universal and existential operators (first two universal and one existential operator, then two existential and one universal operator, etc.), and thus ever richer new forms of language, theoretically an infinite number of them, limited in practice only by unmanageable complexity, result through addition of increasing numbers of operators. This consideration is valuable in that it shows how the structure of a language is determined by arbitrary conventions.

One cannot, indeed, characterize as false the exclusion of unrestricted generality, as performed by the "finitists" Wittgenstein, Ramsey, Schlick and Kaufmann, for the choice of the first, the simplest form of language which they thus make is just as legitimate as the choice of any other form of language. However, this choice is an inconvenient one since it does not correspond to the actual language of science. We find in the language of science formulations of laws of nature, which are assertions of unrestricted universality to the highest degree, and these are used in conjunction with singular sentences, which are undoubtedly "genuine" sentences, as components of implications and conjunctions etc., and hence they are used as genuine statements, not as syntactic rules.[141] It is, therefore, more suitable to choose a form of language containing unrestrictedly universal sentences. In this way the question of the admissibility of such statements receives a clear and complete solution.

There remains, however, the problem of the verification of unrestrictedly universal statements. What led the "finitists" to their elimination from the class of genuine statements was just the circumstance that they cannot be construed as truth-functions of singular statements. It is, indeed, impossible to replace them with finite conjunctions of singular statements, since not all the individual cases to which they apply are known and hence do not admit of complete enumeration and test. It follows that complete verification of unrestrictedly universal statements is altogether impossible. This insight stands irrevocable.

The only way in which unrestrictedly universal statements can be verified is by testing singular statements which are deducible from them in conjunction with other premises, with respect to their agreement with already accepted statements, ultimately observation-reports. If the test comes out positive in all cases and no conflicting statements turn up, then the unrestrictedly universal statement has been verified for these, the known cases; but its validity with respect to the unknown, the future cases remains an open question. For the possibility cannot be excluded that later incompatible singular statements may be found. This partial kind of verification is best designated as "confirmation". (cf. Carnap, T and M, Vol. III, p. 420, 425)

Even though unrestrictedly universal statements cannot be completely verified they can be refuted in terms of an accepted statement incompatible with them. This point has been particularly stressed by Popper. In this connection he called attention to the correlation of universal and existential statements. To a positive universal statement there corresponds the negation of an existential statement, e.g. "all feline carnivorous animals have movable claws" and "there exist no feline carnivorous animals with immovable claws". To the negation of a universal statement there corresponds a positive existential statement, e.g. "not all swans are white" and "there are swans that are not white". A singular existential statement asserts a fact; this property and also its logical correlation to a universal statement makes it fit for purposes of testing. A true positive existential statement, whose negation is the equivalent of a positive universal statement, refutes the latter. Universal statements are thus completely refutable ((falsifiable). This, however, holds only, apart from molecular statements, for universal and existential statements containing just *one* operator, not for statements of more complex form. But then the *negations* of universal statements are verifiable, in terms of a positive singular existential statement—a consequence which Popper, indeed, failed to draw, which was made clear, however, by Carnap.[142] Conversely, in accordance

137

with their correlation to universal statements, existential statements are verifiable on the basis of observation-sentences, but not falsifiable. The statement "there are huge sea serpents" might be verified in terms of a singular existential statement, but it could not be refuted. For it is impossible to undertake a complete search of all oceans in order to ascertain that there are no such animals to be found. Consequently the negation of such an indefinite, non-singular existential statement is not verifiable, though it is falsifiable.

The requirements to be satisfied by a singular sentence, a basic sentence, if it is to be a proper basis of falsification, are accordingly determined by definite logical relations of such a sentence to other sentences:

> "The form of basic sentences must be determined in such a way that (a) no basic sentence is deducible (without special boundary conditions) from a universal sentence, but that (b) a universal sentence can be contradicted by a basic sentence. (b) is satisfiable only if the negation of the contradictory basic sentence is deducible from the theory. From this, together with (a), it follows that we have to determine the logical form of basic sentences in such a way that the negation of a basic sentence cannot itself be a basic sentence.

We have already acquainted ourselves with sentences whose logical form differs from that of their negations: by the operation of negation universal sentences are obtainable from general existential sentences, and conversely, but their logical forms are different. An analogous construction is applicable to singular sentences likewise; the sentence "there is a raven at space-time position k" has a different logical—not just linguistic—form from the sentence "there is no raven at space-time position k". A sentence of the form "there exists such and such at space-time position k" or "there occurs such and such an event at k" we shall call a *singular existential sentence;* and the negation of a sentence of that form, . . . , a *negative singular existential sentence.*

We stipulate that basic sentences are to have the form of singular existential sentences. In that case they satisfy requirement (a), for it is impossible to deduce a singular existential sentence from a universal sentence, i.e. a general negative existential sentence; and likewise they satisfy requirement (b), which is evident from the fact that by omission of the space-time determination a general existential sentence is deducible from any given singular existential sentence, sentences of this form being capable of contradicting a theory". (Popper, *op. cit.,* p. 58)

There exists, then, an asymmetry between verifiability and falsifiability: we have complete falsifiability but not complete verifiability and thus not complete, but only partial decidability of questions of validity. But even partial decision is possible only under certain conditions. A contradiction between a universal and a singular proposition can be avoided, not just in the primitive manner of simply refusing to accept an incompatible singular proposition, but by the introduction of auxiliary hypotheses which show that the contradiction is merely apparent and which thus eliminate it, as illustrated, e.g., by the Lorentz-FitzGerald contraction hypothesis in connection with Michelson's experiment; or by modifying the assumptions in such a way that the contradiction disappears. For in order to test any assertion, be it universal or singular, additional premises, universal or singular, must always be presupposed. These premises can always be modified so as to remove the contradiction, e.g. if we change the coordinating definitions. This point has been emphasized especially by the conventionalists. If measurements of an empirical triangle (like the well known measurement performed by Gauss) yielded an angle-sum different from two right angles, the hypothesis of the Euclidean nature of empirical space would not be refuted if one made the assumption that the light rays along which the triangle is sighted are curved instead of straight.[143] Thus it is only an entire *system* of propositions that can be confirmed or disconfirmed, and a single proposition (a new hypothesis) is capable of confirmation and disconfirmation only if the remaining part of the system is regarded as secure and permanent. But if we do not wish to give up empiricism in favor of conventionalism, we must allow this way of solving contradictions between a consequence of the hypothesis being tested and an accepted basic sentence only under definite conditions. We must not allow the introduction of arbitrary auxiliary hypotheses or modifications of our presuppositions which serve no other purpose than to remove these contradictions and are otherwise unfounded. Such remedial assumptions are arbitrary if they are not either capable of independent verification, in terms of new observations, or deducible from propositions already established. <u>Such are the methodological rules through which empiricism is promoted and validated.</u>[144] They are not arbitrary stipulations but are necessary because uniqueness of factual knowledge and a maximum of order result only if they are observed.[145]

Not all hypotheses or theories are testable in the same measure. Their degree of testability is proportional to the number of possibilities of falsification implicit in their meaning. <u>Popper attempted to determine exactly the relative degree of testability (falsifiability) in two ways: First,</u> by a comparison of the classes of falsification-possibilities of two statements. One statement has a higher degree of falsifiability or testability than a second, if the class of its falsification-possibilities contains the class of falsification-possibilities of the second as a proper part. The two statements have equal degrees of falsifiability if the mentioned classes are equal. If, however, the two classes are related in neither one of these ways, if the classes of falsification-possibilities are incommensurable, then this kind of determination is impossible. Popper tried to obtain <u>a second method</u> of measuring degrees of falsifiability by selecting a class of sentences characterized as "relatively atomic". They are defined as those sentences which result by substitution into some arbitrarily chosen sentential function (which contains, e.g., the schema of a measurement reading). If a sentence can be falsified by a conjunction of n different sentences of a class of such atomic sentences, but not by a conjunction of n-1 such sentences, then the number n represents the degree of complexity of the sentence with respect to this class of atomic sentences; at the same time it represents the degree of falsifiability of the sentence if the atomic sentences are basic sentences.[146]

<u>In this way it becomes possible for Popper to give a</u> <u>precise formulation of the concept of simplicity.</u> This concept played a fundamental role in empiricist thinking since Kirchhoff, appearing in Mach and Avenarius in the form of <u>"conceptual economy"</u>, and current likewise in conventionalist writings since Poincaré. <u>Simplicity is</u> <u>supposed to determine the choice of an hypothesis or</u> <u>theory.</u> But all previous attempts to define the nature of such simplicity and to formulate a measure of simplicity had failed. Sometimes simplicity was characterized from a practical standpoint (like "conceptual economy"), sometimes from an esthetic standpoint, at any rate from an extra-logical platform. <u>Popper, now, tried</u> <u>to define the *logical* meaning of "simplicity" in terms of</u> <u>the degree of falsifiability.</u> It must be said, though, that his brief discussion of such a concept of simplicity does not sufficiently clarify how the concept might be applicable, and that this remains a problem in need of more thorough investigation.

3. *Truth and Confirmation*

<u>As an universal proposition about facts is not com-</u> <u>pletely verifiable, its validity can be established only by</u> <u>verifying each and every proposition deduced from it.</u> This procedure never enables us to secure final validity for such an universal proposition; the latter can only count as being confirmed by a number of tests, and the possibility always remains that a future test might refute it. <u>Therefore we cannot ascribe truth to a universal propo-</u> <u>sition</u>. It may be true, but whether it is true can never be known. On the other hand, the asymmetry between verifiability and falsifiability makes it possible to know

that such a proposition is false, as it is refutable. Hence, if the propositions we talk about are universal we must replace the concept of truth by the concept of confirmation.

The matter is not quite as clear in connection with singular and particular propositions. Such propositions often seem to us to be true beyond doubt.

We feel absolutely sure that our utensils consist of such and such substances, that our apartments have such and such a number of rooms, that the objects we see in front of us are of such and such a kind; in brief, we feel absolutely certain that our interpretations of our perceptions are correct, and any doubt about these matters would be derided as pedantry. Such is our subjective feeling of conviction. But the latter is merely a psychological matter. Is epistemological certainty also possible? The claim that this kind of certainty is attainable must surely be qualified. Such indubitable assertions as were alleged are always about familiar situations, about the customary environment, about objects and classes of objects with which we have intimate familiarity. What produces the feeling of certainty is the fact that judgments of this sort have been tested innumerable times and have always been verified. If, on the other hand, our singular assertions are about new, unusual, strange situations, we feel less certain, and we first have to make certain, i.e. we have to test our assertions.

If we regard a proposition about a repeatedly tested state of affairs as indubitable, this is because we presuppose that things have not changed in the meantime, that there is uniformity in the world, i.e. that there are laws in the world.[147] But this presupposition itself cannot be

143

known to be true with certainty as it is itself an unrestrictedly universal proposition, and thus involves predictions about the unknown, which is beyond possible knowledge. That the unexpected will not happen, we cannot know for certain. It is an article of faith, so firm that we even risk our life on it, but it is not a proposition that could be proved. If we presuppose uniformity, then repeatedly tested and confirmed propositions about familiar situations are certainly true since they are logically deducible from that presupposition. But thus they are but *conditionally* true, not absolutely true. Epistemologically, indeed, such particular propositions have no privileged position; they are not indubitable, and owing to their logical dependence upon universal propositions which are in principle uncertain, not being capable of being definitively established as true, they are in principle no more certain than the latter. If the question of the *evidence* for their truth arises, we have to admit that, like the general presuppositions, they can only be confirmed to the highest possible degree.

Singular propositions are tested by just the same method as universal propositions: consequences are deduced from them which are tested by comparison with accepted basic sentences. To test *all* of the deductive consequences is likewise impossible and hence complete verification is out of the question even for singular propositions.[148]

Just as different propositions have different degrees of testability, so one may be better confirmed than another. The degree of confirmation increases with the number of confirming tests, but it does not depend so much on the *number* of cases than on the degree of rigour of the test. In that case the degree of confirmation depends, indeed, on the degree of testability, but on other factors as well.

The conditions and kinds of confirmation have been discussed more systematically and with superior precision by Carnap.[149] He distinguishes testability and confirmability of propositions. A proposition is confirmable if the conditions can be stated under which the proposition would be true. One proposition may be confirmed on the basis of other propositions, by reducing its confirmation to the confirmation of the latter, either directly or indirectly, completely or incompletely. In general an empirical proposition is confirmable if its confirmation is reducible to the confirmation of an observable predicate. A molecular sentence (i.e. a sentence composed of simple sentences) containing only confirmable predicates is positively as well as negatively confirmable; it is bilaterally confirmable. The same holds of sentences which are formed out of confirmable predicates with the help of sentential connectives (and, or) and operators (universal or existential).

If it is possible to state the circumstances in which a given proposition would be true, it does not follow that these circumstances could actually be ascertained, i.e. that the proposition could actually be tested and is thus practically decidable. A proposition may be confirmable without being actually testable. If we wish to describe a method of testing we must indicate, first, the test-conditions, i.e. a definite experimental situation, and secondly, the truth-condition, i.e. a possible experimental result. This, however, is not enough. The test-conditions must furthermore be realisable. And the fulfilment of the truth-condition must itself be testable. Hence the truth-condition must either be directly described by means of an observable predicate or be defined in terms of such, since the question of the applicability of a given observable predicate is either decidable without indication of a test-method or else a relevant test-method must be specified.

We can now determine to what extent these conditions may be essentially met by the various kinds of propositions. Propositions for which these conditions are formulated in terms of atomic or molecular propositions are *completely* confirmable and also completely testable. On the other hand, propositions whose test-conditions are formulated in terms of sentences containing universal or existential operators, are but incompletely testable and confirmable. The larger the number of operators contained in the formulation of a proposition, the more incomplete the latter's confirmability. It is only affirmative existential propositions and negations of universal propositions of the simplest form that are completely testable. This is just the reason why Wittgenstein and his followers wanted to admit only molecular sentences and to exclude unrestrictedly universal sentences. And this is also why Popper laid down the principle of falsifiability, as it is only the negation of a universal proposition, not the universal proposition itself, that is completely confirmable. But for this very reason the criterion of unilateral falsifiability works only for a language whose sentences do not go beyond the form of universal sentences with one-place predicates; it breaks down for richer languages containing as well existential and universal sentences with many-place predicates.

We are in a position, now, to see clearly in what manner the fundamental principles giving rise to empiricism must be set up. These principles are not truths, they are not statements of fact concerning "the" foundations or conditions of empirical knowledge; rather these principles are postulates concerning confirmability and testability of propositions, and thus concerning the structure of a language. The fundamental postulate of empiricism is that all synthetic sentences and descriptive predicates must be definitely connected with observables. The connection thus postulated may be narrow or broad, strict or rather liberal. The most narrow, strict and radical version of the postulate is the requirement of complete testability of all synthetic sentences. For every descriptive predicate there must exist a method of testing whether the property or relation it designates is or is not attributable to a given space-time position, and such a method must be both known and realisable. This requirement can be satisfied only if, like Wittgenstein, one admits exclusively molecular sentences. The minimal requirement, the most liberal formulation, says that every synthetic sentence must be confirmable, though incompletely only. In between we have various gradations of the requirement with respect to the differences in degrees of testability and confirmability, and also with respect to the difference between complete and incomplete testability and confirmability.

If all that empiricists want is a criterion for delimiting scientific knowledge against transcendent metaphysics, then even the most liberal version of the postulate suffices completely. Metaphysical sentences are not even incompletely confirmable. But at the same time it becomes clear that the possibility of constructing a language for metaphysics is not ruled out. Only, such a language would be one that ignores the requirement of reducibility to observables and thereby shows indifference to procedures of testing and confirming in the scientific sense. Thus it will have to set up alternative criteria of validity. If the metaphysician does not wish to proceed in altogether irrational, intuitive, dogmatic manner but prefers a rational, logical method, he will have to face the task of laying such foundations first.

What, now, is the relation of confirmation to truth? Truth must be distinguished from confirmation. Popper clearly defined the difference between these properties:[150] truth and falsity are timeless, whereas confirmation must always be predicated with respect to a definite time, the predicate "confirmed" must, strictly speaking, always be supplemented by a temporal index. We cannot claim once and for all, with finality, truth for an empirical proposition but must confine ourselves to the statement that it has so far been confirmed. Confirmation is a form of validity capable of degrees, and it can be predicated of a proposition only until further notice, only relatively, not absolutely. No proposition is confirmed absolutely, but only with respect to a certain class of accepted basic sentences. Inasmuch as confirmation is a logical relation between a theory and a set of relevant basic sentences, it is, indeed, itself timeless, but the sum of such basic sentences is not constant, it varies with the time. Hence it does not always remain a logical relation between the *same* sentences, within one and the same system of sentences. This is the reason why truth cannot be identified with confirmation in the manner of pragmatism. The pragmatists are nonetheless right in asserting that only relative confirmation to a higher or smaller degree, not absolute truth, is with certainty predicable of empirical theories or, indeed, empirical propositions. This reasoning led Popper, following the example of Neurath,[151] to the view that <u>the use of the predicates "true" and "false"</u> <u>ought to be discontinued</u> and replaced by the use of "confirmed". He regards confirmation as a distinctive property of empirical propositions which is entirely independent of the concept of truth. Confirmation cannot, in that case, be interpreted as the degree of probability of the truth of a given proposition. If, however, one properly observes the distinction, recently emphasized by Carnap,[152] between <u>truth</u> and <u>knowledge</u> of the truth, then a relationship between confirmation and truth may nevertheless be established, in the sense that <u>confirmation pertains</u> <u>to knowledge of the truth</u>. We cannot know for certain whether a given empirical proposition is true; but its degree of confirmation may be considered as a measure of the probability of its being true.

Although the replacement of the concept of truth by the concept of confirmation is not original with the Vienna Circle—this point of view had already become dominant with the pragmatists—the thoroughness and completeness with which the Vienna Circle investigated the essence of this distinction must nonetheless be acknowledged as an entirely new accomplishment.

4. *Probability*

(a) Logical (propositional) Probability.

As it is only confirmation, not truth, that is ascertainable with regard to empirical propositions, the latter are usually characterized as more or less probable; and the attempt has been made to determine probability degrees with the help of the calculus of probability. The relevant concept of probability, however, is very much in need of clarification, and there has been considerable preoccupation with this problem in the Vienna Circle.[153] The probability of propositions appears to be clearly measurable if it is identified with mathematical probability predicated upon propositions instead of upon events. If in this context mathematical probability is defined as the limit of the relative frequency of two classes of events in the long run,[154] then the probability of a proposition becomes the relative frequency with which a proposition turns out to be confirmed in the class of test cases. In this way the truth-frequency admits of numerical formulation as a fraction.

This conception of probability has been subjected to detailed criticism by Popper.[155] It is above all unclear what propositions are to constitute the series within which the truth-frequency, and so the degree of probability, is to be determined. If such a series consisted of the various basic sentences which either confirm or disconfirm a given hypothesis, then the probability of the hypothesis would still be ½ if even one half, on the average, of the basic sentences disconfirmed it! If, on the other hand, the series consists of the negations of basic sentences which are deducible from the hypothesis (negative existential sentences of the form "there is no A at a place P and at time T which is not a B"), negations, that is, of basic sentences which contradict the hypothesis, and then the proportion of falsified to non-falsified sentences within that series is determined, thus computing falsity-frequency instead of truth-frequency, then the probability would be one even if a certain number of falsifications occurred! For there is an infinite number of negations of basic sentences, of the form "there do not exist . . . ", that are deducible, and only a finite number of them could be falsified. But no other road can be taken if one defines

probability as a proportion of true propositions to false
propositions in a series of propositions. Thus it turns out
to be impossible to determine precisely, by application
of the calculus of probability, the "probability" of a proposition which is supposed to be a measure of its degree
of confirmation. Therefore logical probability must be
distinguished from mathematical probability.[156]

(b) Calculus of Probability

Apart from the question of its epistemological application, the *calculus* of probability has been thoroughly investigated on its own right by the Vienna Circle, especially with reference to its theoretical foundations. This is
due to the fact that the theory of the calculus of probability is itself still controversial—the von Mises theory, the
Reichenbach theory (both forms of the frequency theory), and the theory of ranges are in feud with one another
—and that there are epistemologically significant connections between this theory and the law of large numbers
and the criterion of chance. The calculus of probability,
developed as a formal calculus by means of which new
probabilities can be calculated from given ones, is old.
But the original interpretation of probability as the proportion of "favorable" cases to "equi-possible" cases is no
longer tenable, since "equi-possible" means nothing else
but "equi-probable". The question, then, remains what
exactly is meant by the concept of mathematical probability.

According to one conception, probability means the
limiting value of the relative frequency of an attribute
within a random series. Probability judgements, then,
assert nothing about the individual members of the series
but make an assertion only about the entire series, speci-

fically about the numerical proportion of the occurrence
of the relevant attribute in the series. This interpretation
of the calculus of probability is due to Richard v. Mises,
who developed it carefully.[157] Mises characterized a probability aggregate, a "Kollektiv", by two requirements:
first, randomness, and secondly, convergence of the relative frequency to a limiting value, i.e. a value approached
more and more closely the longer the series.

Feigl,[158] as well as Waismann,[159] criticized these requirements on the ground that convergence to a limit
signifies a certain regularity, viz. that beyond a definite
position in the series the differences from the average
relative frequency remain smaller than some arbitrarily
selected number, however small. Convergence and irregularity (randomness) are thus incompatible requirements. Convergence towards a limit can be asserted only
of such series as are constructed by means of a function
(general term of the series) —for a limit is a property of
such a generating function—, and accordingly not of a
series which cannot, owing to the randomness condition,
satisfy such a law.[160] Feigl moreover called attention to
the theoretical difficulty involved in the assertion of convergence of a statistical series. For any deviation (from
the limit), however small, has a computable probability,
negligibly small though it may be, and might conceivably
occur with the corresponding frequency. Consequently
convergence could be assumed even for segments which
deviate considerably from the computed frequency, since
the deviation could be interpreted as a rarity of very small
likelihood which will be cancelled out as the series is
prolonged. Waismann also called attention to a further
fundamental objection against the frequency theory of
probability. The calculus of probability operates with

infinite series. Statistical series, however, are always finite. Hence it is illegitimate to identify a relative frequency with a limit and one cannot define statistical probability as the limit of a series of relative frequencies.

As an alternative to the frequency theory, Waismann (loc. cit.) constructed a rigorous logical foundation for a conception of probability which may be considered as a development, with the help of some ideas of Wittgenstein, of the classical combinatorial theory of probability, initiated already by Bolzano, v. Kries and more recently by Keynes. The classical concept of probability is defined as the quotient of the number of favorable cases to the number of equally possible cases. What is still required is a precise explanation of the meaning of "objective possibility".

If we interpret probability strictly and correctly, we cannot predicate it of an *event*. For there is no uncertainty with respect to the occurrence of an event: whether or not it occurs is uniquely determined. Probability is rather a property of the *proposition* predicting the occurrence of an event on the basis of other propositions. Hence probability is a logical relation between propositions. This relation is, in contradiction to the *strict* deducibility of a proposition from others, its rigorous demonstrability, not completely but only partially determined, and the degree of determination yields the gradation of probability.

Usually a proposition is not determinate or specific to the extent that a unique fact corresponds to it. The fact by which it is verified may vary within certain limits. To the proposition "NN lives in Vienna" there corresponds a multiplicity of possible facts: he might live in this or that section of the city, in this or that house, on this or that floor. <u>What is described by a proposition is in most cases only a domain of individual facts, a logical range.</u> The ranges corresponding to two (or more) propositions may be mutually exclusive or one may be included in the other or they may overlap. If, now, we introduce a measure of the sizes of the logical ranges, by means of a suitable convention, then these relations of ranges admit of quantitative, numerical determination; to mutual exclusion we assign the measure 0, to inclusion the measure 1, and to overlap a fraction (between 0 and 1). <u>The probability conferred by proposition p upon another proposition q is the measure of the range of their logical product (p and q) divided by the measure of the range of p.</u> If instead of p we consider the sum-total of known true propositions, we obtain the probability conferred upon q by our total present knowledge. The greater the range of the logical product, the greater the probability. Upon this foundation "all propositions of the calculus of probability admit of purely formal deduction without recourse to additional assumptions". (p. 239).

This interpretation of probability accords well with the fact that probability judgments are called for whenever only part of the determining conditions of an event are known or taken into consideration, such that our knowledge would not warrant a complete, i.e. absolutely determinate assertion. The concept of probability expresses gradated uncertainty with respect to the truth of such an assertion. Nevertheless probability is not merely subjective, for it determines the logical relationship between two propositions. On the basis of the partially known conditions of a class of events a determinate probability is, with the help of a metric for the sizes of logical ranges,

154

computable, and from such a probability predictions of frequencies within statistical series are derivable, provided the conditions are empirically realised. This theory of probability is in the mentioned respect highly superior to <u>the frequency theory of probability</u> which simply has to presuppose statistical series as given. In a certain sense the frequency theory has thus been incorporated into <u>the theory of ranges</u>, although not all the difficulties besetting the frequency theory are thereby eliminated. If experience confirms a probable prediction, this signifies that the events are completely determined by the conditions implicitly specified by the choice of the reference-class and are independent of other, unknown circumstances. If experience, on the other hand, *dis*confirms the probability prediction, then we search for an explanation of the discrepancy in terms of additional determining conditions. In this way probability is connected with dependence of one event upon others, i.e. law and chance. This logical reconstruction of probable inference has been accepted by Carnap[161] and Schlick.[162]

Popper nevertheless continued to adhere to the frequency theory of probability, though not without heeding the objections against the theory and improving the latter's formulation. The improvement consisted in his ingenious idea to formulate the requirement of randomness as a purely mathematical requirement, viz. that the relative frequency of an attribute in a sequence should remain unchanged if we cut out of the original sequence elements in any manner whatsoever with the sole restriction that the method of selection should refer only to the relative positions of the elements. Instead of presupposing irregular statistical series, he thus constructs chance-like *mathematical* series, determined by a rule, which mirror the random nature of chance-series. A sequence of attributes is chance-like, if the limits of the frequencies of the fundamental attributes remain unaffected by elimination of elements on the basis of their positions relative to preceding elements. The postulate of randomness is thus expressed as a frequency hypothesis, and in this manner a purely mathematical foundation has been laid.

But as empirical chance-series are finite, we must abstain, in their mathematical representation, from the postulation of a limit of relative frequencies, since such a limit exists only for infinite series. Popper, therefore, replaces the limit postulate by the concept of an accumulation-point of relative frequencies in a sequence. This means that beyond any given segment of a sequence there are always further segments in which the relative frequency differs from a definite frequency, the frequency determining the accumulation-point, by less than any preassigned number. If a sequence has only *one* such accumulation-point, not several ones, a single mean-frequency which is at the same time the mean-frequency of any subsequence of elements (selected in the manner specified above), then the limit postulate need not be satisfied.[163] Such a unique mean-frequency represents the "probability" of occurrence in a specified reference-class of a given attribute. Thus chance-like series behave like convergent series.

Popper then proves that Bernouilli's theorem does not require the limit postulate and presupposes only invariance of the mean relative frequency with respect to selections of the specified kind. The proof consists in showing that this assumption suffices for proving the theorem also for chance-like sequences *without* limit of the relative frequencies. On the frequency interpretation of probability the Bernouilli theorem asserts the following: the relative frequency of an attribute in a segment of a random sequence differs from the mean frequency of the attribute in the whole sequence by less than any preassigned number, however small, if the segment is sufficiently long—or rather, this holds for the overwhelming majority of such sequences. The smaller the segments, the larger the deviations of the frequencies from the mean frequency; the larger the segments, the smaller these deviations, the closer the behavior of the segment approximates to the behavior of convergent sequences. This, however, is nothing else but the law of large numbers. The latter thus turns out to be a tautological transformation of Bernouilli's theorem and a logical consequence of the definition of the type of series to which the theorem applies, viz. series of events exhibiting a mean frequency which remains unaffected by selections of a specified kind. The paradox is thus solved that in spite of the "irregularity" of such series there results a "law" of large numbers. For it is a purely logical consequence of the mentioned structural property that such a series is still irregular in small segments and that order in the sense of convergence emerges only in large segments.

If one accepts the subjective theory of the calculus of probability, one cannot interpret Bernouilli's theorem as a proposition about frequencies in the sense of the law of large numbers, and hence one is at a loss to explain the applicability of the calculus of chances to statistical series, or the success of statistical predictions. The earlier version of the frequency theory, on the other hand, already *postulated* regularity in large series by the introduction of a limiting value. What Popper did was to deduce the law of large numbers as a *mathematical* theorem. Nevertheless it is applicable to empirical facts in this sense: it expresses mathematically that property of series of events which is meant by saying that they are irregular in small segments and approximate to convergence in large segments. But if the chance character of a series, even of a statistical series, is thus expressible in terms of a mathematical condition of randomness—invariance of mean frequency with respect to selections—, then the validity of the law of large numbers with respect to the series follows logically from the assumption that the series is chance-like; hence the law is necessarily valid for such *empirical* series. The calculus of chances, including the law of large numbers, may thus be looked upon as a mathematical theory of an empirical subject-matter, or putting it conversely: having defined mathematical series of random character, we find that there exist empirical statistical series corresponding to them and hence embodying the law of large numbers. Thus mathematical series and the mathematical law of large numbers are found to be empirically applicable.

Empirical applications of the concept of mathematical probability are neither completely verifiable nor completely falsifiable. Verification is impossible because the propositions of the calculus of chances are about infinite series, while empirically given series are always finite. However close the correspondence between such a series and a mathematical probability judgment, it still remains wholly uncertain and undecidable whether the correspondence would continue to hold as the series is prolonged. What prevents us here from complete verification is the same sort of limitation of our knowledge as was seen to make verification of unrestrictedly universal propositions

impossible. For this very reason, however, no empirical
series could refute a mathematical probability judgment
either. After all, it is of the very nature of a probability-
sequence that deviations from the calculated probability
occur; what needs to be postulated is only that these
deviations will be cancelled out as the sequence is prolonged. Probability judgments are thus theoretically undecidable. They cannot even be empirically confirmed
(loc. cit., p. 194) ; but in that case they would be factually meaningless! Popper concedes (p. 133) that such propositions must therefore be considered as " 'saying nothing about reality' or as 'factually empty' ", though not
necessarily as devoid of logical content; "what speaks,
however, against such an interpretation is the great pre-
dictive *success* achieved by physics with the help of probability-hypotheses".[164] In physics they are thus either
accepted as practically confirmed or rejected as useless,
refuted by experience.

The point may be clarified with reference to the
logical form of probability judgments and the latter's
relation to basic sentences. From probability-hypotheses
consequences can be deduced, specifically existential statements about the members and segments of a series, e.g.
that there are segments in which the frequency of the
attribute in question differs infinitesimally from the
mean frequency. These are *general* existential statements:
"Members of such and such a kind occur again and again;
they are existential hypotheses and hence neither verifiable nor falsifiable". Yet, it is possible to verify corresponding *singular* existence assertions. A probability judgment is confirmed to a greater or smaller degree or not
at all, accordingly as many or a few or none of such existential consequences are verified.

This, however, does not suffice. Probability-judgments must not be used without restriction. For any kind of regularity that might be encountered could always be interpreted as a rare segment of a random series. It is for this very reason, indeed, that probability-judgments are irrefutable. It follows that the use of probability-hypotheses should be limited in terms of a methodological rule. This rule prohibits the assumption of predictability and reproducibility of those segments of a random series whose deviations from the mean frequency are more marked in one direction than in the other.[165] For the very improbability and rarity of such segments makes them unpredictable and unreproducible. In order for a probability-hypothesis to be acceptable as confirmed, merely approximate agreement with basic sentences will not do, but what is required is the best possible agreement within the limits of attainable accuracy of measurement. In this manner probability-hypotheses may be employed just like other kinds of hypotheses.

III. THE DOMAIN OF THE KNOWABLE

1. *Unity of Science, and the Universal Language*

The establishment of the unity of knowledge is a historical task of philosophy.[166] The Vienna Circle likewise did not fail to be aware of this task. One cannot acquiesce in a juxtaposition of the conceptual systems of physics, biology, psychology, sociology and the historical sciences, as though they were incommensurable, and as though in each of these sciences a unique language were spoken. If the various special sciences are considered as heterogeneous in subject-matter, method and criteria of validity, then they appear unrelated, especially the natural sciences on the one hand and the social sciences on the other hand, and it is not clear how the concepts and laws of one science are related to those of another science. But one cannot avoid borrowing concepts and laws from one domain for use in another. If one is to explain, and not just describe, a process like perception, this is possible only by going beyond the conceptual system of psychology, since such a process must be brought into relationship with a physical stimulus and a physiological process. Any prediction, however, involves this sort of integration of different scientific domains, being a process with complex conditions. The derivation of a prediction, an activity of supreme importance, presupposes, therefore, the utilization of laws from diverse sciences, laws of nature as well as laws of human behavior. But if so, then the laws and concepts of the special sciences must belong to *one* single system, they cannot be simply juxtaposed without connection. They must constitute a unified science with one conceptual system (a language common to all the sciences) containing the conceptual systems of the individual sciences as members and their languages as sublanguages.[167]

The language of unified science must satisfy two requirements: it must, first, be intersubjective, i.e. from the formal point of view it must constitute a common system of signs and rules, and from the semantic point of view, a given sign must have the same meaning for any language user; secondly, it must be universal, i.e. any sentence of any language whatever must be translatable into it; it must constitute a conceptual system in which any state of affairs whatsoever can be expressed. Carnap and Neurath believed at first that the language of physics satisfies the conditions of a conceptual system of the specified kind, for which reason this theory has been named "physicalism".

The statements of physics describe the properties of space-time positions quantitatively, but qualitative predicates, as ascribed to the objects of the perceptual world, may likewise be included in the language of physics provided they can be coordinated to physical states or processes. This is the reason why Carnap modified the thesis of the unity of science[168] to the effect that the unification is not in terms of the conceptual system of physics but in terms of observable properties and relations of things. The name "physicalism" thus becomes unsuitable and should be replaced with "thesis of the reducibility of scientific language to the thing-language". It is not the quantitative language of physics but the qualitative thing-language which constitutes the unified language of science. What this means is that all statements, whatever their subject-matter may be, are reducible to statements about states of, or processes in, the world of material objects. Thing-predicates do not belong exclusively to any one sense-domain: the vibrations of a tuning fork are not only audible but also visible and tangible. Thing-predicates are intersubjective. Quite on the contrary, however, a given sense-quality is coordinated with a unique bodily process. To a given tone there correspond vibrations of a definite fundamental frequency and definite overtone frequencies, and of definite amplitude. It is, therefore, possible to characterize sense-qualities uniquely in terms of physical relations, and this is why statements about the former are translatable into statements about the latter. Ascertainment of physical relations is independent not only of definite sense-domains but also of definite observers. It is always theoretically possible to obtain agreement between different people about states of and processes in the world of material objects, just because this world is an intersubjective one. It follows that the thing-language, the language used to describe observable properties and relations, is itself intersubjective.

It is not only the domain of physics but likewise the domains of all the other natural sciences that can be described by means of this language. Even if there should be irreducible laws of biology, in other words, even if not all the *laws* of biology should be reducible to the laws of physics, it remains the case that the biological *concepts* are ultimately reducible to observable properties and relations of material objects. If such concepts as "dominant drive" or "entelechy" do not admit of such reduction, this is because no testable consequences are deducible from hypotheses formulated in terms of concepts of this sort. But for this very reason such concepts are wholly inadmissible in science.

2. *Physicalism*

The statements of the natural sciences are anyway statements about spatio-temporal situations involving things. The statements belonging to other domains must at least be translatable into statements of this kind. Mathematics and logic admit of expression in such a language insofar as they are treated as pure calculi, combinations of mere symbolic patterns. The real problem of the "physicalistic" language of unified science, however, is whether even the domain of mind is describable by means of such a language. What is here in question is the translatability* of psychological statements into statements about bodily states and processes. In order to lay the foundations for such translatability, Neurath and Carnap formulated a thesis which may be characterized as "physicalism" in a narrower sense.

At first, they looked upon psychological and physical statements as two different kinds of statements in the sense that psychological statements are about experiences considered as non-physical events. Thus Carnap says, in his first article[169] about the problem, quite unambiguously: "One may verify under what physical conditions he *experiences* . . . a given quality"; or, the responses, here, "may be partly so-called physical processes, partly mental processes; if, now, the above mentioned thesis that psychological concepts and propositions are reducible to physical concepts and propositions is valid, then we have to do in all cases with physical processes" (p. 451). Accordingly the fundamental thesis is clearly expressed as follows:[170] "The thesis of physicalism should not be interpreted to prescribe to psychology exclusive occupation with physically describable states of affairs. What is rather meant by the thesis is that, although psychologists are free to investigate whatever matters they wish and to formulate their propositions in whatever manner they desire, these propositions are in any case translatable into the physical language". After all, it does not make sense to speak of translatability of psycholog-

---

Translator's note: Kraft's discussion of "physicalism" evidently refers only to relevant publications before Carnap's *Testability and Meaning* (Philosophy of Science, 1936/1937). Accordingly the important distinction between "translatability" and "reducibility" is not observed at all. For a formulation of physicalism as a thesis of *reducibility*, see Carnap's "Logical Foundations of the Unity of Science", Int. Encyclopedia of Unified Science, I, 1, 1938.

ical statements into physical statements unless these are different kinds of statements to begin with.

This dualistic conception, however, is at the same time repudiated when the inference is drawn "that all the statements of psychology are assertions about physical processes (in the body and specifically in the central nervous system of the subject concerned)".[171] The scientific content of statements about mental phenomena can consist in nothing else but statements about bodily states. For it is only the latter sort of statements that are intersubjective and testable. If statements about mental phenomena are interpreted as non-physicalistic, then they are in principle untestable, since the life of mind is not publicly observable. Accordingly, non-physicalistic statements about mental phenomena are explicitly ruled out of the language of science. "If we speak dualistically—as is almost invariably the case in philosophy—of 'qualities of experience' and also 'physical states of affairs' (. . . of the mental and of the physical . . .), then contradictions are inevitable".[172] Beliefs about mental states of another person are merely inessential associative imagery. The logical content of statements about mental phenomena is exhausted by statements about physical states of affairs. "There exist fundamentally but one kind of objects, viz. physical events".[173] Statements of empirical science cannot be about anything but material objects,[174] for such statements alone are intersubjectively intelligible and testable. Consequently traditional psychology must be replaced by a radical behaviorism as the only possible form of scientific psychology. "Psychology is a branch of physics".[175] Statements about mental states, dualistically interpreted, are thus scientifically meaningless, i.e. devoid of theoretical content. The assumption that behind the bodily behavior of people there are mental states does not even admit of a formulation in physical, and hence scientific language. It represents a mere pseudo-statement. It is metaphysics. Thus the original thesis was turned into a far more radical contention.

This radical physicalism has, more than any other tenet of the Vienna Circle, repulsed philosophers and encountered vigorous opposition from the very start. But the thesis seems to be an inevitable, rigorous logical consequence of the postulate of verifiability. Here as elsewhere the significance of such uninhibited radicalism lies in its opening up legitimate and important questions.

It is impossible to verify directly a statement about another mind. For unowned mental states cannot be directly observed. If, with Scheler, one should maintain that mental states like anger, joy, embarrassment can be directly read off a person's face, then "to read off his face" means just "to base one's psychological diagnosis upon facial expressions, and thus upon bodily processes". Such a judgment always presupposes the presence of linguistic communications or bodily expressive symptoms or a general way of behaving in the cognitive situation. Without such signs contained in the physical world, verification of statements about other minds would be altogether impossible—except on the assumption that telepathy occurs. And this holds not just for present unowned mental states but also for the past states of one's self. If, however, every statement about mental states must be logically justified in terms of statements about bodily states, then a statement about the physical world must be co-ordinated with every psychological statement, and thus it appears to be possible to eliminate psychological statements altogether and to replace them with the coordinated statements about the physical world. For, owing to this correlation the mental can be described in terms of the coordinated physical. In this way the mental is not, to be sure, *definable,* but the extensions of concepts of mental states can thus be uniquely determined. But for this very reason psychological statements are equivalent to the corresponding "physical" statements, they have the same theoretical content. There is, in that case, no theoretically relevant, or even theoretically describable, difference between them. Hence statements about mental phenomena must, if they are to be considered scientific, be translatable into statements about the physical which alone are testable. Radical physicalism is thus radical behaviorism. There are no meaningful, non-physicalistic statements about mental events. "Psychological" statements have a testable meaning only if they are physicalistically interpreted. Looked at in this light, the radical thesis of physicalism becomes not only intelligible but even apparently inevitable. Let us, however, be clear as to what exactly is entailed by radical physicalism. Statements about unowned mental states in the sense of non-physical events are meaningless pseudo-statements since they are in principle unverifiable. This implies that even people's assertions about their own mental states are, from an intersubjective point of view, unintelligible and meaningless if they mean anything else than bodily states. "If the sentence 'A was angry yesterday at noon' is devoid of meaning for me, since . . . I could not possibly verify it, then the fact that an acoustic event exemplifying the pattern of this sentence issues from the mouth of A does not make it any more meaningful".[176] All that the sentence could significantly refer to are acts of bodily behavior, specifically "verbal" behavior.

But in the ultimate analysis even statements about one's own experiences can mean, in the intersubjective language of unified science, nothing but bodily phenomena, unless they are to be unverifiable. "Yesterday I got excited" means only "my body was yesterday in that physical state which is commonly called 'excitement' ".[177] Thus the language of experience-protocols becomes a "sublanguage of the physical language".[178] But the implication of this position is the collapse of the solipsistic basis of the constitution-system. The concepts of the world of things cannot any more be constituted by an ordering of experiential data, but on the contrary the constitution-system must be built upon a basis of "physical" concepts, or more specifically "thing-concepts". The conception of the foundations of empirical knowledge has thus undergone a radical transformation, from the doctrine of the immediacy of states of consciousness to materialism.

It would not be pertinent to criticize this physicalistic thesis, as is usually done,[179] on the basis of the dualistic *presupposition* that there are mental events which are distinct from the processes occurring in the respective organism. One rather ought to examine the physicalist claim that psychological statements interpreted in *this* way cannot even be formulated in scientific manner, i.e. in such a way as to render them testable.

The fundamental question which ought to be raised first of all if one wishes to launch a critique of radical physicalism, is: how is it at all possible to talk about other minds in scientific, intersubjectively intelligible manner? How is it at all possible to form in scientific manner the concept of the mental as something non-physical? For as unowned mental states are inaccessible to direct observation, it is impossible to think of them as isolated, separate from their bodily symptoms. Such, indeed, is the basic argument of physicalism. What is denied is not the existence of mental events but rather the possibility of meaningful talk about them. For they are metaphysical postulations, statements about them are meaningless, in principle unverifiable. If psychological statements "mean" mental states, then such "meanings" are but associative imagery which has nothing to do with the theoretical content of statements.[180] It is therefore impossible to state in intelligible language the difference between a statement about 'mental' phenomena in the ordinary sense and a statement about the corresponding bodily process.[181] The concept of the "mental" in the usual sense cannot, according to physicalism, be scientifically formulated at all.

But here the question arises, first of all, what is the exact status of the concepts of the thing-language, the concepts forming the physicalistic reduction-basis. We require a set of indefinable primitive concepts of the thing-language. These primitive concepts do not admit of *ostensive* definition either. For what can be directly given is not intersubjective, and therefore not physical. The given consists of subjective percepts—unless one should pay homage to naive realism, that confusion of physical objects with subjective percepts. But surely, it could not be maintained that the concepts referring to the world of things are epistemologically so clear and unproblematic that they could be presupposed without further analysis as the logical basis of science. The concept of a "physical object" has been reduced from secondary qualities to primary qualities, and from the latter to measurable values of physical state-variables, at which point the epistemological problem arises just what the object of physical knowledge is: extra-mental realities like electrons etc., with their "complementarity" of particles and waves of matter, or just correlations of sense-data.[182] It is thus apparent that the concepts of the thing-language represent a problematic presupposition, and hence one can hardly introduce them without further ado as undefined primitive concepts.

In order to constitute the concept of the "mental" in the ordinary sense, all we need to presuppose is what everybody is familiar with in terms of his own experience. Its qualitative side is not communicable, for the intersubjective content of assertions is "structure", ordinal relations of the qualitative contents to one another.[183] But the subjective terms of these intersubjective relations are indispensable and uneliminable. It is these subjective contents of experience which constitute the facts serving as a basis for the construction of an intersubjectively intelligible concept of the mental. It is the concept of the general nature of the data of experience, a nature common to experiences of color, of cold, of pain, of aversion, etc. These qualities are intersubjectively determined by their structural definition, although the qualitative contents may vary from individual to individual. The general concept of something of similar kind as that which each one of us lives through, of something functioning as a qualitative filling of intersubjective relations, is thus capable of intersubjective constitution.

But it must further be shown how the mental is communicable. In fact, it already suffices for the demonstration of the intelligibility of statements about other minds, to point out that unowned mental states are determined by their ordinal (structural) relations, that the latter differentiate them sufficiently and determine them uniquely.

Such structural relations, however, are all that is needed to make intersubjective communication possible. Whenever I receive a communication, I may fill the structure with contents of my own experience and thus at the same time form an image in my mind of the general nature of the mental states of other people. Thus I understand what is meant by the communication: something of the same nature as the color I myself experienced or the pain I felt myself, though it may not resemble the latter exactly.—Statements about mental events, interpreted non-physicalistically, are thus meaningful.

Nevertheless, such a concept of the mental would be useless, because dispensable, if to every mental process there corresponded a bodily process, a process not just postulated but actually ascertainable. For in that case it would indeed be possible to speak throughout of the parallel bodily processes instead of the mental processes, as the corresponding assertions would be equivalent; whenever one is true, the other is true also.

The next pertinent question to be discussed in a critique of radical physicalism, therefore, is whether what is usually considered as a mental state can, indeed, be completely characterized in terms of statements about bodily conditions, and whether accordingly psychological statements could be replaced by the latter kind of statements. Such a program of physicalistic description, however, encounters fundamental difficulties. There are a great many mental phenomena (in the usual sense), above all in the domain of thinking and imagination but also in the domain of perceptions and organic sensations, for which scarcely any bodily expressive symptoms are known, and if there are any such symptoms, they are most unreliable or altogether inadequate for a detailed description. The fact that a person has a definite thought, a definite memory, a definite wish, a definite visual sensation, as a rule does not manifest itself at all, or only vaguely, in his behavior, and hence it could not be described with approximate, not to mention complete, specificity in behavioral terms. And as regards the correlated processes in the central nervous system, they are not known in detail. The only evidence we have for the truth of statements asserting such mental facts are the statements made by the subjects having the experience.

In order to be able to describe such mental phenomena in physicalistic language, Carnap had to take recourse to an indirect method of description of the coordinated bodily states, making use of expressions designating mental states. He characterizes such a state as that state of the body which occurs when the subject makes an assertion about a definite experience, where by the "assertion" is meant nothing but a physical event (sounds, written words). The event, e.g., of somebody seeing red is physicalistically described by characterizing the bodily state of the respective person as a state of seeing red. "Seeing red", however, means in this usage, not a sensation, but a class of bodily reactions (lingual movements, gestures such as pointing at a red object) which regularly follow upon certain stimuli (questions, taken as verbal sounds, or as series of written marks). The reference to the mental event "seeing red" is supposed to be replaced, in the description, by reference to a *bodily* state "being in a state of seeing red"; and this bodily state is characterized in terms of its connection with a definite class of reactions of the red-seeing subject.[184]

In order to characterize a given mental phenomenon

172

uniquely in physical terms, one would have to be able to specify *all* reactions that might serve as signs of the respective bodily state. For if this were not possible, then it might happen that while a person is actually in a given mental state one is forced to infer that this mental state does not occur. The reactions in terms of which the bodily state "seeing red" could be determined may consist in differently worded assertions in different languages, or they may consist in gestures of pointing at all sorts of red objects. But it is also possible that no such reactions occur at all, for it is not necessary that all sensations be expressed. And as for the cerebro-physiological processes, they are not sufficiently known. It is reasonable to assume that the reactions in terms of which the bodily state "thinking of proposition p" ("p" may be replaced by "$2 \times 2 = 4$", e.g.) might be determined are very scarce— if there are any at all. But even whatever rare reactions may occur will entirely lack specificity. They may be sighs of thinking in general, but will be useless for inferences to the specific content of the proposition thought about. A psychological statement is not equivalent to a *single* physical statement but only to a conjunction of physical statements. But such a conjunction of possible bodily reactions cannot be completely and sufficiently determined by a class defined in terms of a property or relation, nor by enumeration. The only way the class can be defined is by saying that it comprehends just the bodily expressive symptoms for a definite class of *mental* phenomena. But exactly what bodily states belong to such a class of expressive symptoms, cannot be predicted at all. Such knowledge is precluded by the unforeseeable multiplicity of variability of such symptoms.[185] This multiplicity can be unified only in terms of coordination to a kind of experience. <u>The mental in the usual sense is thus ineliminable.</u>

This is most emphatically true of that fundamentally important kind of mental event called "<u>understanding of signs</u>". The understanding of a meaning is not[186] "completely determined by the physical properties of the stimuli affecting our sense-organs". If a flag-signal is given on a ship, all physical (optical) stimuli are identically presented to all persons on board; but the signal is understood by the crew, or at least by a part of the crew, while it is not by the majority of the passengers. This is because the interpretation of the stimulus depends not only on <u>the properties of the stimulus</u>, the object functioning as sign, but also on <u>the background of learning of the interpreter.</u> The meaning of a sign must have been learned before the sign can be understood. It is this latter, <u>the subjective condition,</u> which makes it necessary for Carnap to take the interpreter into account in his attempt at physicalistic analysis of the concept of understanding. According to Carnap, what characterizes a sign or a meaningful act as understood is the fact that a subject reacts to it in terms of an appropriate protocol sentence. The role played by the subject in this connection is merely that of an organic detector; the subject's experience of understanding is not mentioned at all in the description, but only the verbal utterance expressing understanding. In this way, Carnap believes, the description does not refer beyond the domain of the physical, for an assertion is considered by him as a physical event (sound or inscription).

<u>But the physical event as such will not do. It in turn must be understood.</u> For it is impossible to specify all.

possible combinations of sounds or written marks through which a given act of understanding may be expressed. Even though there may not be an infinite number of them, they are at any rate unforeseeable. The *experience* of understanding could be dispensed with only if it were possible, not only to give a physiological definition of the learning process, in terms of the formation of condition-ed reflexes, but also to uniquely describe in detail what has been learned in such physicalistic fashion. As long as this cannot be done, it is impossible to circumscribe or characterize or define the act of understanding in purely physicalistic terms. And in the meantime the mental re-mains as an indispensable and ineliminable non-physical phenomenon. The physical language, or thing-language, thus fails for the description of the mental. And for this reason the traditional dualism of mind and body, and therewith the dualism of the language of experience and the thing-language, stands unshaken.

The situation, then, is this: if one should hold that the concept of the "mental" in the usual sense cannot be constituted and that meaningful statements about mental events are impossible, then scientists will have to abstain from a large quantity of assertions they currently make, and in that case the major portion of the social sciences would have to be discarded.

In order to place given actions into a causal or teleo-logical order, one must relate them either to their psycho-logical motives or to the latter's bodily correlates. Our knowledge of the latter, however, is far from being suf-ficient for inferring them from given actions. The psych-ological connections, on the other hand, are much better known. Hence we have to depend upon psychological motivations if the bodily processes correlated with them are unknown. Such, to a large extent, is the situation in historical inquiry and also in judicial inquiries.

But how, now, can statements about other minds in this non-physicalistic sense be intersubjectively tested in those cases where no direct bodily signs for the mental states are given? We are confronted with this kind of situation when, to give an illustration, the question is raised in a court whether the violent death of a given person should be regarded as a case of premeditated murder or as a case of manslaughter (unintentional killing). If the intent to kill is well concealed, then direct bodily signs of such a motive (statements made by the murderer) are lacking. In order to discover a design, one takes the entire situation into consideration, with the question in mind whether it could have motivated a design to murder. Such inferences may be drawn from deliberated actions. The latter may be actions which by themselves are no evidence for intent to murder but acquire such a meaning only within the total context, such as, e.g., the context of previous inquiries about the presence and absence of certain persons. Or one might infer from a state of extreme irritation of the suspect that it was merely a case of manslaughter. Such inferences are based, on the one hand, on the fact that actions issue out of motivational contexts, that they are elements in a psychological causal nexus of ends and means to their realisation. On the other hand, they are based on purely psychological laws, like the law that a highly affective state excludes deliberation and implies a vehement impetus towards action. Conclusions about unowned mental states, such as somebody else's intentions, are thus founded upon psycho-physical laws (like the correlation of actions and purposes) and intra-psychological laws (like the negative correlation of affective state and deliberation). These laws are the result of induction from one's own and other people's experience, and their employment as means of interpretation of other people's behavior has again and again led to their confirmation. It is such laws which make an intersubjective test of statements about other minds possible, even though we may have no direct bodily signs of the states of other minds to go by. Even psychological states of affairs which are but indirectly connected with observable bodily conditions according to psychological laws (the latter may be no more than statistical laws, probability-implications), may be validly inferred. Statements about other minds are legitimate scientific statements.

Thus we cannot maintain the thesis that the physical language, or the thing-language, is fit to serve as the universal language of unified science. For statements about mental states and processes are not translatable without remainder into this language. The language of experience and the thing-language, the conceptual system of the mental and that of the physical, stand autonomously side by side. Science cannot dispense with one any more than with the other.[187]

3. *Reality*

The domain of the knowable is determined by the conditions of confirmability. Confirmation of an empirical proposition necessarily reduces to perception, ultimately to one's own perceptions. Indeed, even knowledge about other than one's own experiences is based on one's own perceptions; I have to hear or read the reports of other persons. But it does not follow that only first-person experience is knowable, nor that knowledge is limited to

experience in general, to data of consciousness, as has
been claimed by positivism. It cannot be denied that
even in the Vienna Circle there have been times when
some members would identify reality with data of experience.[188] According to Carnap's constitution-system
of concepts the meaning of statements can consist in nothing else but correlations of the given, correlations of perceptual data in the case of statements about physical objects, and similar correlations in the case of statements
about other kinds of entities. The fear of metaphysics was
a preventive against any attempt at transcending the
domain of experience. But this conception has been entirely abandoned with the advent of physicalism, and
Schlick repudiated explicitly and in detail identification
of his epistemology with any sort of theoretical idealism
or solipsism, in his own essay "Positivismus und Realismus".[189]

It is a complete misunderstanding of the doctrine
defended by the Vienna Circle that all propositions,
including those about reality, must be testable and confirmable by experience, to take it to assert that only sense-
data are real, that physical objects are nothing but
auxiliary constructs for ordering sense-data, that the
external world is nothing but a "logical construction" in
a sense in which this implies its unreality. This position
was actually endorsed by some positivists, though it was
at times merely read into positivism. J. Stuart Mill's
definition of material objects as "permanent possibilities
of sensation" leaves one undecided whether Mill does or
does not hold this view. Insofar as the given is considered
as the content of somebody's consciousness, the assertion
of the exclusive reality of the given leads to the assertion
of the exclusive reality of states of consciousness; there

exists, then, nothing beyond consciousness. If, more specifically, the view is that the given is distributed over a plurality of conscious subjects, we have idealism; if, however, the given is restricted to what is given to me, the result is solipsism. Either doctrine, however, is metaphysical. For what is thus asserted is that nothing exists beyond the empirical world, no transcendent being behind the phenomena. But such an assertion does not admit of empirical test and decision, no more than the thesis of metaphysical realism according to which there exists beyond the empirical world another, absolute world; whether the latter be held to be knowable in some special way or whether it be held to be unknowable, does not matter.

Consciousness, however, enjoys no privileged position as regards *empirical* reality. The point is not that the given is neutral, as in Mach and Avenarius, and that the mental as well as the physical is a logical construction out of data as neutral elements; the important point is rather that a state of consciousness, a feeling, a pain, can be said to be objectively real in no other sense than a physical object. "To be real always means to fit into a definite nexus with the given" (loc. cit., p. 105). For this interpretation alone makes statements about reality testable and confirmable.

Objective reality cannot be guaranteed by a single event but only by a causal order. If the question should arise whether there is a pain in this or that part of my body, in the appendix or in the liver, then symptoms for such a pain will have to be found (by touching or similar operations). And in just the same way the reality of *unowned* states of consciousness may be ascertained. For example, one may verify in terms of invariable connections between bodily and mental processes that a given person is really happy—or, for that matter, that he is not really happy. Linguistic expressions, communications from the other person, bodily expressive symptoms, familiarity with the other person's character and with his momentary condition—all of them represent connections between observable bodily states and (for me) unobservable mental states, the latter being assumed as real in spite of their unobservability, though such assumptions are but hypothetical—like all empirical propositions.

And by just the same method the reality of unobserved or even unobservable physical objects and events is established. If they are postulated on the basis of natural laws connecting them with observable facts, if they can be fitted into the spatio-temporal system of the external world, then such assumptions are just as valid as propositions about observed physical objects and events. "We have, therefore, definite empirical criteria for determining whether houses and trees already existed when we did not see them, and whether they already existed before we were born and will continue to exist after we die, in other words: the assertion that those objects exist independently of us has a perfectly clear, testable meaning and must, of course, be accepted. We can without difficulty define the difference between those objects and those which exist but 'subjectively', 'dependent on ourselves' ".[190] In this sense of "reality", there can be no doubt about the reality of the other side of the moon[191] nor about the fact that the planets will continue to move in their orbits even after the extinction of all consciousness.[192] And similarly the reality of atoms and electric fields is established in terms of the uniformities revealed by physics. "Logical Positivism and Realism are thus not in opposition".[193] "The formulation, employed by some positivists, that physical objects 'are merely complexes of sensations' must therefore be repudiated".[194] These words express a clear and unambiguous endorsement of empirical realism. Not that this amounts to the assertion, or the denial of the existence of a transcendent, absolute reality, for such a reality cannot be intelligibly talked about.[195]

To be real means empirically: to fit into the spatio-temporal system of the intersubjectively observable. Whether this system itself is nothing but a conceptual construction or whether it represents an absolute reality subsisting by itself, this question cannot even be formulated. It is the problem of the "transcendent ideality or reality" of space and time—a metaphysical problem. Whether what we accept as real is "truly" real, whether what we accept as existing independently, outside of our consciousness, is really an independent reality, or whether no absolute, "independently existing" reality corresponds to our beliefs—this is evidently a metaphysical question, a question going wholly beyond the domain of the scientifically knowable. The meanings of "reality" and "existence" in this usage cannot even be defined since no empirical criterion of such "reality" can be stated. It is for this reason that such sentences about metaphysical existence have been called meaningless.[196]

What would it be like to find out whether an absolute reality corresponds to empirical reality or whether there does not? A reality which is not given in immediate experience can be no more than an object of thought, something believed in or postulated, and nothing else. The usual procedure is to make a hypothesis concerning a reality independent of our experience and to state definite testable criteria for it, in that definite observation-sentences are implied by an existence assertion. Any question concerning empirical reality, e.g. whether a mountain in some unknown territory is real or merely legendary, is conclusively decidable in terms of sensory evidence. But now we can hardly set over against the conceptually postulated reality outside our consciousness another reality which is not likewise a conceptual postulate. Just how should one arrive at such absolute reality? It is nonsensical to demand that our assumption about reality be measured by such a standard of absolute reality. With regard to absolute reality or ideality there is no possible decision procedure. It is for this reason that the question concerning the reality or ideality of the external world has been characterized as a pseudo-problem, being interpretable only as a metaphysical question. For the thesis of the *empirical* ideality of the external world, i.e. that the real is coextensive with the contents of consciousness, cannot be maintained, and the thesis of the empirical reality of the external world is a necessary hypothesis. All historical theses concerning ultimate reality, metaphysical idealism and metaphysical realism, phenomenalism, solipsism, even the older positivism with its restriction to data of consciousness, are theses transcending the domain of scientific knowledge. For the question they attempt to answer cannot possibly be answered.

4. *Values*

Problems of value have also been dealt with by the Vienna Circle, though only to the extent that they admit of scientific discussion. Carnap, indeed, was a radical in this context too, in that he excluded value judgments entirely from the domain of theoretical discussion. He held that the specific content of value judgments does not admit of theoretical formulation. "Either empirical criteria are laid down for the use of 'good', 'beautiful' and the rest of the predicates employed in the normative sciences, or not. On the former alternative, sentences containing such a predicate turn into empirical statements of fact, but not value judgments; on the latter alternative, the sentence turns into a pseudo-statement; it is impossible even to formulate a genuine statement expressing a value judgment."[197] Further, "the objective validity of a value or a norm cannot (even in the opinion of axiologists) be empirically verified or deduced from empirical propositions; hence it cannot even be meaningfully asserted" (ibid.) [198]

These claims are still based on the original definition of meaningfulness in terms of verifiability, which was subsequently felt to be too narrow by Carnap himself. According to this criterion, indeed, descriptive sentences alone can be meaningful since they alone are verifiable. All other sentences, such as questions, commands, rules, valuations, are meaningless, but only in the sense that they have no representative, or theoretical content. If, on the other hand, meaning is defined pragmatically, then sentences of these kinds may also be meaningful. For they refer to definite attitudes or forms of behavior. To value judgments, specifically, there correspond empirically specifiable objective relations (between properties of objects and attitudes).[199]

The task of laying the foundations of ethics was undertaken by Schlick.[200] The possible scientific achievements of ethics are limited to the description and systematization of moral norms, but no norms are posited in scientific ethics. Ethics can validate derivative norms in terms of fundamental norms, but it cannot *justify* the most fundamental norms, it can only describe their acceptance as a fact. There are no criteria for absolute values, all values are relative to a subject. On the other hand, ethics can *explain* norms on the basis of general, extra-ethical conditions; it can deduce moral attitudes from the natural laws of behavior in general.

Schlick accepts as a general law of motivation the hedonistic law that volitional decisions are determined by the motive with a maximum of positive hedonic quality or a minimum of negative hedonic quality. "Good" in the moral sense is a predicate referring to volitional decisions and expressing approval by the society. What forms of conduct are morally approved of by a society, and why they are thus approved of, is determined by the pleasant and painful consequences for the society of given forms of conduct, or more accurately, by the society's *beliefs* about such consequences. An individual acts morally because what is useful from the point of view of society may be pleasant for the individual himself. Such regard for pleasant consequences is produced by educational suggestion and by penalties and rewards instituted by the society; the causes of socially responsible behavior are thus external in either case. However, conduct in conformity to social demands may also become intrinsically and immediately pleasant for the individual. The sympathetic sharing of other people's happiness is likewise a possible source of pleasure, and in this way not just egoistic behavior but also altruistic behavior acquires value. Nevertheless, the hedonistic analysis of value cannot ignore the fact that suffering is not always a negative motivation inasmuch as sacrifice is often valued more highly than happiness. Schlick accounts for this apparent exception to hedonism by saying that in such cases suffering is either itself a necessary condition for pleasure or else is a complex state containing pleasure as a component since suffering as a highly affective state may itself be pleasant.

Schlick advocates an ethics of kindness in contrast to an ethics of duty. It is an ethics of the "beautiful soul" who desires from inclination what the society sets up as a duty. This must be regarded as a goal, to be approached by the process of evolution, whose attainment is far off in the future. In the meantime an ethics of duty alone has practical significance as the past as well as the present prove.

In my "theory of value" I endeavored to show in detail that hedonism is inadequate for the explanation and justification of values.[201] Values do not exclusively stem from the quest for pleasure and absence of pain. There are also other, equally important, sources of value. Such a source is above all aptness to satisfy biologically conditioned needs, drives, desires. The determining factor here is not imaginative anticipation of pleasure resulting from satisfaction, but the immediate drive and its consummatory termination.

My "theory of value" contains a comprehensive investigation of the realm of values and of the foundations of scientific statements about values, and my endeavor was to clarify value problems both in psychological and in logico-theoretical respects. Most normative concepts, with few exceptions such as the most general ones ("valuable", "excellent" etc.), have besides their specifically normative character also a descriptive content.[202] It is the latter which is specified by definitions of normative terms, as e.g. in the definition of "morally good" in terms of conformity of the will to a moral law or in terms of a will directed to universal happiness or in terms of a sympathetic heart, or in the definition of "beautiful" in terms of an harmonious organization of parts within a whole. In this manner value judgments acquire a factual, theoretical content. Hence value judgments—and the same holds for norms—admit not only of psychological but also of logical analysis. Owing to this factual content, value judgments are capable of standing in logical relations to one another; the class-relations of the concepts in terms of which they are formulated set them into relations of subsumption, some value judgments can be recognized as inconsistent with others, some are logically deducible from more general value judgments.[203] These logical relations constitute the foundation of systems of ethics and esthetics on the one hand, and of all rational criticism on the other hand. Whatever value judgments are thus deducible are, however, conditional only. They always presuppose other, more general, value judgments.

The source of the specifically normative quality, of that which characterizes the good and the beautiful defined in such and such a way as "valuable", is a certain *attitude* towards the defined factual content. Such attitudes may be friendly or hostile, they may be desires or aversions, approvals or disapprovals. Value qualities express such attitudes, they are non-theoretical, signals for practical action. Thus the predication of value is seen to be meaningful; we know the conditions of applicability of value predicates.

A value judgment consists in the attribution of value to an object or a class of objects. Value judgments are thus wholly meaningful, not just as regards their descrip-

186

tive content — if meaning is not restricted to descriptive meaning.[204]

A value judgment, however, does not merely express the personal attitude of the judging individual, but functions also motivationally as persuasion of the hearer to share the speaker's attitude. For a value judgment does not limit itself to subjective expression, it further claims universal validity.

However, such invitations to share the speaker's attitude, which are expressed by value judgments, need not be accepted. There is no authority that would compel universal acceptance of such imperatives, the way the acceptance of descriptive statements is compelled by the process of verification. For there are no absolute values nor a categorical imperative, but only hypothetical values. The values that are believed to be absolute are nothing but those values and imperatives which have become a matter of course in a given cultural community. Specific value judgments can be deduced as objectively valid only if one presupposes fundamental norms that are universally accepted. This holds for all objective criticism, for this is the only sense in which the objective validity of value judgments can be maintained—conditional validity of derived value judgments. Considered as unconditional assertions of absolute values, based on no presuppositions whatever, no value judgments can claim universal validity. Such a claim cannot be justified in any way.

5. *Philosophy*

The postulate that philosophical method should be scientific was the most basic postulate of the Vienna Circle, the very foundation of the Circle's unity. There was agreement with the tenet of positivism that philosophy does not investigate a special domain of reality. As regards *empirical* reality, that is the concern of the special sciences; and non-empirical, transcendental reality is no possible object of knowledge. The traditional subject matter of metaphysics, absolute being, as well as absolute values and norms, cannot constitute a special domain of knowledge. For questions and assertions about such a domain are wholly devoid of factual content, they are but pseudo-questions and pseudo-statements. Philosophy in the sense of metaphysics does not admit of scientific treatment.[205]

But it was not equally clear what the positive conception of philosophy was to be. In a programmatic paper, introducing the first volume of "Erkenntnis",[206] Schlick developed a new conception of the task of philosophy which may be traced back to L .Wittgenstein. It is the task of philosophy to clarify the meanings of words and statements and to identify and eliminate nonsensical statements. Accordingly philosophy does not establish specifically philosophical propositions but only clarifies given propositions. Philosophy is not a system of truths and therefore does not constitute a special science; rather it consists in "that activity by which the meanings of propositions are ascertained or clarified. Philosophy clarifies propositions, science verifies propositions. The latter is concerned with the truth of propositions, the former, however, with the question what exactly propositions *mean*".[207] In this sense, philosophy is not a science with a subject-matter of its own, but a method which is employed in the special sciences whenever and wherever there occur obscurities. We thus confront the paradoxical result that progress towards scientific solidity undermines the very *raison d'être* of philosophy conceived as a science.

In Carnap's works, however, philosophy has been more precisely defined as "the logic of science", logical syntax of the language of science. There are two comprehensive realms, the realm of objects, their properties and relations, and the realm of *representation* of objects, i.e. of language and logic. The whole of the realm of objects belongs to the special sciences, which deal with it exhaustively. The realm of philosophy is that of *representation* of objects: it is the concepts, propositions, theories of science which constitute its subject-matter. Wittgenstein was the first one to define philosophy in this way.

In the "Logical Syntax of Language" Carnap defined the task of philosophy as the investigation of the logical syntax of language. Philosophy consists partly of statements about such syntactic structure, partly of quasi-syntactic or pseudo-object statements (see earlier, p. 74 f.) We frequently find a similar situation in foundation problems of the special sciences. These problems are formulated as questions about the world of objects, but their analysis reveals that they are questions about language, about syntactic relations. Such so-called philosophy of nature, of organism, of mind, of history, should be interpreted as logical analysis of natural science, of biology, of psychology, of historical science. The foundation problems of physics, as e.g., the problem of the structure of space and time, were by Carnap interpreted as questions concerning the syntax of space- and time-coordinates. The foundation problems of biology, which concern predominantly the relation of biology to physics, are questions concerning the translatability of the language of biology into the language of physics. Likewise the foundation problems of psychology, e.g., the psycho-physical problem, are problems concerning the relationship of two sub-languages of the universal scientific language, the psychological and the physical language, such problems as "whether two parallel sentences of the latter languages have always, or in certain cases, identical content".[208] Again, the foundation problems of mathematics, such as the issue of formalism vs. logicism, concern the structure of a formal system which pervades the entire language of science. Since syntactic problems admit of purely formal treatment, abstracting from any reference to meanings and confining itself to relations of symbols, it follows from this conception that the propositions of philosophy can be expressed in purely formal manner. Schlick, on the contrary, followed Wittgenstein in identifying philosophy with analysis of the meanings of scientific propositions.

Yet, as has been mentioned already (p. 77), Carnap has in the meantime abandoned this syntactic conception of philosophy. If philosophy is logical analysis of the language of science, then philosophy is not concerned with the syntax of the latter, for logic is not a matter of syntax but a matter of semantics. Logical analysis, then, cannot be divorced from attention to the semantic dimension of language, and the purely formalistic study of language is thus abandoned. Philosophy conceived as logical analysis of the language of science does not, in that case, differ significantly from epistemological analysis of the sciences. It comprehends any topic dealt with in non-psychological epistemology and addresses itself to all the problems connected with the foundations of the special sciences. The latter class of problems have been extensively discussed in the Vienna Circle: discussion of the epistemological foundations of mathematics at the meeting in Koenigsberg 1930,[209] of the relevance to biology of

quantum-physics at the preliminary conference at **Prague,**
1934,[210] of the problem of causality,[211] of the concept of
the whole.[212] The problems of traditional philosophy can
either be formulated as empirical problems, in which
case they belong to the special sciences, or as problems
of representation, language, meaning or also syntax, or
else they are metaphysical questions which preclude any
scientific investigation.

The sort of conception of philosophy which the
Vienna Circle has advocated is by no means a radical in-
novation. Kant already limited philosophy, considered
as a cognitive discipline, to epistemology,[213] and the positivists already left all responsibility for factual knowledge
to the special sciences. What makes, however, the Vienna
Circle's conception superior to the positivist conception
is the idea of the unity of science. For thus the problems
of a unified world-view, which constituted a primary concern of the philosophies of the past, remain as scientifically legitimate problems in the form of problems of
a unified system of scientific knowledge. And further it
was in the Vienna Circle that the method of epistemology
was precisely defined as logical analysis of language.
Knowledge is based on designation, representation, on
language, and therefore the analysis of knowledge must
be performed by means of linguistic analysis.

The traditional concerns of philosophy fall into three
groups: first, questions about empirical facts; their solutions must come out of the factual sciences. Secondly,
questions concerning representation, language; these
questions must be settled through clarification of concepts and propositions. And thirdly, there were the metaphysical questions; such questions cannot be answered
at all, since they cannot even be formulated in the lan-

guage of science, in terms of scientific concepts. Thus, none of the meaningful, scientifically legitimate problems of traditional philosophy are discarded.

If now, we survey in retrospect the philosophical accomplishments of the Vienna Circle, we find that the latter are results which led the theory of knowledge far beyond its stage of development at that time. The nature of logic and mathematics was clarified, the relation of logic to language was even revealed for the first time, and the methods and foundations of empirical knowledge were analyzed and clarified with a thoroughness without precedent. It cannot be denied that these accomplishments were accompanied by quite a few oversimplifications and one-sided, radical views which have not yet been entirely superseded. After all, the work of the Vienna Circle has not been finished, it has been interrupted. The movement of neo-positivism which was initiated by the Vienna Circle will continue the work. But it cannot be denied either that new and fertile ideas came out of the Vienna Circle and that their discoveries represent deep insights and clarifications of great value. At a time when metaphysical tendencies and dogmatic constructions dominated German philosophy, the members of the Vienna Circle were doing philosophy in a scientific spirit. They cultivated their studies in the spirit of clarity, thoroughness and solidity which is demanded by the scientific method, in contrast to the usual vagueness and instability of philosophical claims; that their approach had a scientific soberness about it instead of appealing to the heart and fulfilling secret wishes, was indeed inevitable. Imaginative conceptual poetry is surely more interesting for the average person, and the wisdom of a great personality surely has more significance for human life. Yet, they are subjective, matters of opinion, unverifiable. Lacking universal validity, they are matters of personal conviction, but do not represent knowledge.

Notes Part One

1. cf., Wissenschaftliche Weltauffassung. Der Wiener Kreis. Vienna 1929. Also Neurath, Den logiska Empirismen och wiener kretsen, 1936 (Theoria, V. II, p. 72 f.)
2. For a bibliography of the participants, see "Wissenschaftliche Weltauffassung", 1929; also "Erkenntnis", V. I, p. 315 f., and "Einheitswissenschaft", H. 1, p. 30; H. 3, p. 21, 22.
3. This is evidenced, e.g., by Schlick's explicit statement, in the essay "Meaning and Verification" (Gesammelte Aufsaetze, p. 340), that he owes his definition of meaning to discussions with Wittgenstein which strongly influenced his own views in this matter. "I can hardly exaggerate my indebtedness to this philosopher".
4. Political tendencies, such as Neurath occasionally injected into publications and such as the "Vienna Circle" was reproached for by Dingler in the preface to his "Grundlagen der Geometrie" (1933), had nothing to do with the aims of the "Vienna Circle", which were purely philosophical. Reichenbach repudiated such tendencies (Erkenntnis, V. 4, p. 75 f.), and likewise Professor Schlick emphatically disowned them in conversations with me.
5. See the report of the congress in Erkenntnis, V. 2, p. 86 f.
6. A bibliography of these schools is contained in Erkenntnis, V. 5, p. 199 f.
7. For a report of the preliminary conference in Prague, see "Einheit der Wissenschaft", 1934. For a report of the first congress in Paris, see "Philosophie Scientifique", Paris, 1935, and "Actes du Congrès internat. de philosophie scientifique" (Actualités scientifiques et industrielles, No. 378-395, Paris 1936). There is a report of both sessions in Erkenntnis, V. 5, p. 1 f., p. 377 f. The following publications were intended as introductions to this congress: Vouillemin, La logique de la science et l'école de Vienne; Neurath, Le développement du cercle de Vienne et l'avenir de l'empirisme logique. Both published in Paris, 1935.
8. Already published in part, as "International Encyclopedia of Unified Science", Chicago, 1938 and following years.
9. Report in Erkenntnis, V. 6, p. 275 f., and in "Das Kausalproblem", Leipzig and Kopenhagen, 1937.
10. Report in "Zur Enzyklopaedie der Einheitswissenschaft", Haag, 1938.
11. Report in Erkenntnis, V. 7, p. 153 f.
12. It is not true, therefore, that Carnap "emigrated to America", as G. Lehmann puts it in "Die deutsche Philosophie der Gegenwart", 1943, p. 293.
13. Documented in the periodicals "Philosophy of Science", Baltimore 1930

and following years, and "Journal of Symbolic Logic", Baltimore, 1936 and following years.

14. Documented in the periodical "Analysis", Oxford, 1933 and following years.

15. Publicized in the periodical "Theoria", Lund, 1935 and following years.

16. With "Studia Philosophica", Lemberg, 1934-38, as organ of publication.

17. Russell, "Logical Positivism", 1946 (*Polemic*, V. I). On p. 7, the Vienna Circle, "which afforded a rare example of fertile cooperation among philosophers", is referred to, together with the Warsaw school, as being "of the highest caliber". "The school deserves admiration for its resolution to do philosophy in scientific manner, for its unyielding love of truth and for its technical work in logic, syntactics and semantics". "But in spite of the great merits of the school, it suffers from a certain narrowness and blindness for some problems of considerable importance", such as problems of psychology and others (p. 12).

18. Thus Weinberg, in "An Examination of Logical Positivism" (1936), adds to some criticisms the following compliment: "Nevertheless, the investigations into logic, mathematics, and the nature of scientific systems, conducted by the logical positivists, are of the utmost importance. It seems justified to assert that these studies have yielded the clearest insights so far into logic and scientific systems, and it is this which must be regarded as the most illuminating merit of logical positivism" (p. 294). And Petzaell says on p. 36 of "Der logische Positivismus" (1931, Goeteborgs Hoegskolas Arsskrift, 37): "In spite of the reservations here expressed, we believe that a revision of the language of science, such as the Vienna Circle of the Scientific World-View endeavors to undertake, will be of extraordinarily high value".

19. This attitude is taken by Heimsoeth, in his new edition of Windelband's "Lehrbuch der Geschichte der Philosophie", 1935, where he says (p. 574): "Man, Spirit and History are looked at from the vantage point of a methodological and epistemological dogma which allegedly does not presuppose any ontological dogma, and are thus ultimately misunderstood in all essentials". Also by Del Negro, in "Die deutsche Philosophie der Gegenwart", 1942, p. 8: "Neopositivism has declared violent war not only on metaphysics but on philosophical endeavors in general". It "tries to lend to its claims the appearance of unsurpassed exactness by dressing them up in logistic cloths. The only novelty as compared with Mach lies in the formalistic domain". And by Gerh. Lehmann, in "Die deutsche Philosophie der Gegenwart", 1943, who mentions only Carnap (see the quotation later on p. 102), and again by Bochenski, Europaeische Philosophie der Gegenwart", 1948, p. 62 f. The evaluation given by E. v. Aster, "Die Philosophie der Gegenwart", 1935, p. 177 f., constitutes the only exception to this negative attitude.

20. Gesammelte Aufsaetze, 1938, p. 390.

21. Ibid., p. 391.

22. Ibid., p. 394.

Notes Part Two

1. See, e.g., Schlick's polemic against Neurath's radicalism with respect to philosophy in the monograph "L'école de Vienne et la philosophie traditionelle", 1937 (Gesammelte Aufsaetze, p. 391, 392, 395); and Neurath's polemic against Schlick's "Konstatierung" in: Radikaler Physikalismus und "Wirkliche Welt" (*Erkenntnis*, vol. 4, 1934, p. 346 ff.)
2. First published under the title "Logisch-philosophische Abhandlung" in "Annalen der Naturphilosophie", 1921.
3. cf. p. 24, note 17.
4. Carnap, Die alte und die neue Logik, *Erkenntnis*, V. I, 1930-31, p. 12 f.; K. Menger, Die alte und die neue Logik, 1933, in *Krise und Neuaufbau in den exakten Wissenschaften*, Heft I; Joergensen, *A Treatise on Formal Logic*, V. I, 1931.
5. Carnap, *Foundations of Logic and Mathematics*, 1939. (International Encyclopedia of Unified Science, Vol. I, No. 3.) p. 37, 66.
6. e.g., Bross and Bowdery, A realistic criticism of a contemporary philosophy of logic, 1939 (*Philosophy of Science*, vol. 6, p. 105 f.); cf. V. Kraft, Logik und Erfahrung, 1946 (*Theoria*, vol. 12, p. 205 f.)
7. cf. Hahn, *Logik, Mathematik und Naturerkennen*, 1933 (Einheitswissenschaft, H. 2), and in *Erkenntnis*, V. 1 (1930-31), p. 97 f., V. 2 (1931), p. 135 f. The view that logic and mathematics assert nothing about the world but consist of transformation-rules and internal relations of symbolism, derives originally from Wittgenstein.
8. Hahn in *Erkenntnis*, V. 2, 1931, p. 137.
9. When Schlick (*Gesammelte Aufsaetze*, p. 145 and 222) makes this point by saying that mathematics deals only with combinations of "symbols", it should be understood that what the symbols designate are just groups of units, or more precisely: classes of classes (or sets).
10. cf. V. Kraft, Mathematik, Logik und Erfahrung, 1947.
11. Couturat, Les principes des mathématiques, 1905. Die Prinzipien der Mathematik, 1935.
12. Brentano, *Versuch ueber die Erkenntnis*, ed. by Kastil, 1925.
13. Schlick characterizes the insight into the nature of logic, into "the relationship of logic to reality and experience", as the "most important step in philosophy" (*Gesammelte Aufsaetze*, p. 223).
14. See C. W. Morris, The Relation of the Formal and Empirical Sciences within Scientific Empiricism, 1935 (*Erkenntnis*, V. 5, p. 6 f.)
15. As, e.g., by G. H. v. Wright, in *Den logiska empirismen*, Helsingfors, 1943.

16. *Gesammelte Aufsaetze*, p. 342: "I would prefer to call it consistent empiricism".
17. *Testability and Meaning*, p. 422: "The name 'scientific empiricism' is perhaps appropriate."
18. Morris, "Logical Positivism, Pragmatism and Scientific Empiricism", 1937; Petzaell, *Der logische Positivismus*, 1931; Weinberg, *An Examination of Logical Positivism*, 1936; Blumberg & Feigl, *Logical Positivism*, 1931 (*Journal of Philosophy*, 28).
19. Kaila, *Der logische Neopositivismus*, 1931; similarly, Aster, *Die Philosophie der Gegenwart*, 1935.
20. *Testability and Meaning*, p. 422.
21. A more detailed study of the historical background of neo-positivism may be found in Weinberg, loc. cit., p. 2 f.
22. cf. Carnap, Die Aufgabe der Wissenschaftslogik, 1934 (Einheitswissenschaft, H. 3); Carnap, Von der Erkenntnistheorie zur Wissenschaftslogik, (Actes du Congrès internat. de philosophie scientifique, Paris, 1935. I. Philosophie scientifique et Empirisme logique, 1936); Carnap, Die Methode d. log. Analyse (Actes du 8e Congrès intern. de Philos. 1936, p. 142 f.); Waismann, Was ist logische Analyse? (*Erkenntnis*, V. 8, 1939-40, p. 265 f.).
23. Carnap, Die Aufgabe der Wissenschaftslogik, 1934, p. 6.
24. Carnap, Die Methode der logischen Analyse (Actes du 8e Congrès internat. de Philosophie à Prague, 1943, 1936), p. 124 f.
25. The points of view from which language may be studied have been distinguished by Carnap as "pragmatic", "semantic" and "syntactic" *Introduction to Semantics*, 1942.
26. *Tractatus logico-philosophicus*, 1922, p. 78.
27. loc. cit., p. 188: "My assertions are illuminating by the fact that he who understands them will finally recognize them as nonsensical".
28. cf. Schlick, Meaning and Verification, 1936 (*Gesammelte Aufsaetze*, p. 338 f.), and compare with Lewis, Experience and Meaning, 1934 (Phil. Review, Vol. 42). (The two essays here mentioned are reprinted especially for purposes of comparison in Feigl & Sellars, *Readings in Philosophical Analysis*. Translator's note.)
29. This formula is due to Wittgenstein, whose "Tractatus logico-philosophicus" has been the starting-point for the Vienna Circle's theory of meaning and meaninglessness.
30. cf. Carnap, Ueberwindung der Metaphysik durch logische Analyse der Sprache, 1931 (*Erkenntnis*, V. 2, p. 219 f.)
31. cf. Schlick, Unanswerable Questions, 1935 (Gesammelte Aufsaetze, p. 369 f.)
32. cf. Schlick, *Gesammelte Aufsaetze*, p. 222: "5+7=12 is not a statement at all, it is a rule permitting us to transform a statement containing the symbols 7+5 into an equivalent statement containing the symbol 12. It is a rule regarding the use of symbols". (Instead of "statement" we should put, in the last two occurrences, "formula", in order to avoid

inconsistency with the use of "statement" in its first occurrence). "The rules of arithmetic are tautologies; they do not express some kind of knowledge. The same holds with regard to all logical rules".

33. *Tractatus logico-philosophicus*, p. 188. Schlick likewise often uses sentences for which he asks to be excused in view of their meaninglessness, with the purpose of calling attention to a certain point.

34. A. Petzaell, *Logistischer Positivismus*, 1931, p. 34, 35 (Goeteborgs Hoegskolas Arskrift, vol. 37.)

35. Actes du huitième Congrès internat. de Philosophie, 1936, p. 203 f.

36. Weinberg, *An Examination of Logical Positivism*, 1936, p. 195.

37. Lewis, Experience and Meaning, 1934 (*The Philosophical Review*, V. 42).

38. Nagel, Verifiability, Truth and Verification, 1934 (*The Journal of Philosophy*, vol. 31).

39. Stace, Metaphysics and Meaning, 1935 (*Mind*, vol. 44).

40. Reichenbach, *Wahrscheinlichkeitslehre*, 1935.

41. *Logik der Forschung*, 1935 (Schriften z. wissenschaftlichen Weltauffassung, V. 9), p. 21.

42. *Philosophy of Science*, vol. 3, 4, 1936-37.

43. cf. Carnap, *Foundations of Logic and Mathematics*, 1939 (Int. Encyclopedia of Unified Science, V. I, No. 3). Schaechter, *Prolegomena zu einer kritischen Grammatik*, 1935 (Schriften z. Wissenschaftlichen Weltauffassung, V. 10). Schlick, Form and Content, 1932 (*Gesammelte Aufsaetze*, p. 152 f.)

44. cf. Carnap, *Foundations of Logic and Mathematics*, p. 11.

45. Even Schlick, who used to define meaning in terms of verifiability, was once led to this conclusion (Gesammelte Aufsaetze, p. 157): "The meaning of a sentence results automatically once the vocabulary and the grammar of the language is known".

46. This is actually an old insight. As alleged by H. Bergmann (*Zur Geschichte und Kritik der isomorphen Abbildung*, in: Actes du Congrès international de philosophie scientifique. VII., p. 67) on the basis of a hint by Kuntze (*Erkenntnistheorie*, p. 64), it was stated already by S. Maimon, who asserts (in his "Streifereien", p. 100) in connection with Leibnitz (Nouveaux Essais, Livr. II, Chap. 9), that in communication the matter of subject and predicate is left out completely and only the form is kept. Also Poincaré pointed this out, likewise Russell (*Introduction to Mathematical Philosophy*, p. 83).

47. Schlick, while aware of this point, did not express it clearly, but rather created the opposite impression by using "ausdruecken" ("express") only from the point of view of communication (p. 159, 169, 177: "incommunicability as the criterion of inexpressibility"). But he himself distinguished sharply between "expression" and "representation" (p. 154).

48. Schlick, *ibid.*

49. Schlick, indeed, expressed this with unmistakable clarity. *Ibid.*, p. 194, 205.

50. Schriften zur wissenschaftl. Weltauffassung, V. 8; English transl., London, 1937.
51. According to O. Kraus (Wege u. Umwege der Philosophie, 1934), Wittgenstein was first stimulated in this direction by Brentano's and Marty's philosophy of language (see Carnap, Die Aufgabe der Wissenschaftslogik, 1933, pp. 24, 25.)
52. Die logische Syntax der Sprache, p. 6.
53. The method of arithmetization, an exact method for such investigations, was introduced by Goedel, a former participant of the Vienna Circle (Ueber formal unentscheidbare Saetze der Principia mathematica u. verwandter Systeme, 1931, Monatshefte f. Mathematik u. Physik, Jg. 38.)
54. At present, though, Carnap puts less emphasis on the distinction between derivation and consequence, since he has discovered in the meantime that for both the same procedure of constructing a sequence of sentences may be employed.
55. It is only the concept "analytic" which comprehends everything that is valid on the basis of logic alone, while the concept "provable" comprehends only what is logically derivable; which does not exhaust all logical relations.
56. *Ibid.*, p. 36.
57. Das Kontinuum, 1918.
58. Tractatus logico-philosophicus, 1922.
59. The most important forerunner is Tarski's "Fundamentale Begriffe der Methodologie der deduktiven Wissenschaften", 1930 (Monatshefte f. Math. u. Phys., Jg. 37).
60. Schlick, *Gesammelte Aufsaetze*, p. 320.
61. By this time, however, Carnap has recognized the insufficiency of these definitions as applicable to any kind of calculus, and revised them with the help of new syntactic concepts in "Meaning and Necessity", 1947.
62. Survey of Symbolic Logic, 1918.
63. Introduction to Semantics, p. 249, 43.
64. Philosophy of Science, vol. 4, 1937, p. 25.
65. This was emphasized for the first time by K. Menger in the controversy about the foundations of mathematics (Der Intuitionismus, 1930, in *Blaetter f. deutsche Philosophie*, Jg. 4), and thereafter K. Popper endorsed this point of view as a regular tenet of the logic of science (*Die Logik der Forschung*, 1935, p. 19 f., 195). The term "principle of conventionality", presently preferred by Carnap (*Introduction to Semantics*, p. 247), is more suggestive of the essence of the position.
66. Der logistische Versuch einer Neugestaltung der Philosophie (Actes du 8e Congrès internat. de Philosophie, 1936, p. 203 f.)
67. Tractatus logico-philosophicus, p. 188.
68. The Concept of Meaning in Pragmatism and Logical Positivism (Actes du 8e Congrès de Philosophie à Prague 1934, 1936, p. 102 f.)
69. A Survey of Symbolic Logic, 1918.

70. Joergensen likewise maintained the indispensability of intensional logic: Ueber die Ziele und Probleme der Logistik, 1932 (*Erkenntnis*, V. 3, p. 73 f.)

71. In his "Logical Syntax of Language" already Carnap had recognized that the construction of logical formalism requires a logic which pays heed to meanings, since in order to determine logical relationships we have to interpret assertions about the marks and formulae of the meta-language materially, in accordance with their meanings.

72. cf. Carnap, Formalwissenschaft und Realwissenschaft. *Erkenntnis*, Vol. 5, p. 36.

73. Carnap, *Die logische Syntax d. Sprache*, p. 177, 211.

74. The connection between the modalities and the logico-syntactic forms of sentences was first recognized by Wittgenstein.

75. O. Becker, Zur Logik der Modalitaeten, 1930 (Jahrbuch der Phaeno-menologie, V. 11). Lukasiewicz, Untersuchungen ueber den Aussagen-kalkuel, 1930 (Cont. Rend. de la Société des Sciences de Varsovie, V. 23, Cl. III, 1930).

76. Tractatus logico-philosophicus, p. 84.

77. Carnap, Ueberwindung d. Metaphysik durch log. Analyse d. Sprache (*Erkenntnis*, V. 2, p. 228).

78. In "Testability and Meaning", V, IV. See earlier, pp. 40, 41.

79. Introduction to Semantics, 2nd ed., 1947, p. 250.

80. *Introduction to Semantics*, p. 249.

81. For a critical discussion, see Petzaell, in *Theoria*, 1936, p. 359 f.

82. Die logische Syntax der Sprache, p. 206, 207.

83. Carnap, *Log. Syntax d. Sprache*, p. 210.

84. From Carnap's statement (L.S.d. Sp., p. 210, 260) that logic of science is no special discipline, no new discipline coordinated with the special sciences (or with the unity of science), since pure and descriptive syntax are nothing "but mathematics and physics of language", one might be inclined to infer that it is thus at least a new branch of mathematics, like group theory.

85. *Introduction to Semantics*, p. 245.

86. Mill, *System of Logic*, book II, Chap. 2., sec. 2.

87. Logische Syntax der Sprache, p. 211.

88. "S_1 is called a sentence in the material mode of speech, if S_1 predicates a property of an object, for which there is a distinct, and specifically syntactic property which is, so to speak, parallel to it, i.e. which is predicable of a designation of the object if and only if that property is predicable of the object itself" (Carnap, L.S.d.Sp., p. 213). "E.g., the sentence S_1: five is not a thing but a number. Apparently this sentence attributes a property to the number five, just like the sentence 'five is not an even but an odd number' (S_2). In reality, however, S_1 is not about five but about the word 'five': this is shown by the formulation, of identical content with S_1: (S_3) 'Five' is not a thing-word but a number-word. While S_2 is a genuine object-sentence, S_1 is a pseudo-object-sen-

tence; S_1 is a quasi-syntactic sentence (of the material mode of speech), and S_3 the parallel syntactic sentence (of the formal mode of speech)" (ibid., p. 211).

89. *loc. cit.*, p. 234, example 48.

90. *Ibid.*, example 43.

91. "All such pseudo-questions disappear once we employ the formal instead of the material mode of speech, by using, that is, corresponding syntactic words (numerical expression, spatial coordinate, predicate) in place of universal words (number, space, universal)" (L.S.d.Sp., p. 238).

92. *Ibid.*, p. 227, example 21.

93. *Ibid.*, Example 22. Weinberg (*An Examination of Logical Positivism*, 1936, p. 250) also emphasizes that "the question concerning the nature of number . . . can be regarded as a question concerning the analysis of mathematical terms in the *object*-language".

94. Testability and Meaning, *Philosophy of Science*, Vol. IV, p. 5.

95. Testability and Meaning, VIII, p. 429.

96. Carnap, Der logische Aufbau der Welt, p. 150. Similarly, Schlick, Gesammelte Aufsaetze, p. 147.

97. Schlick, loc. cit., p. 227.

98. Carnap, *Erkenntnis*, V. 2, p. 436.

99. Hahn, Logik, Mathematik u. Naturerkennen, p. 17.

100. *Erkenntnis*, V. 4, p. 419. See also Kaila, Rudolf Carnap: Logische Syntax der Sprache, 1936 (*Theoria*, V. II, p. 83 f.).

101. cf. in this connection the critical remarks on p. 109.

102. Der logistische Neupositivismus, 1930 (Annales Universitatis Aboensis, Ser. B. Tom. XIII).

103. Erkenntnis, V. 2, p. 77.

104. Die Anarchie der philosophischen Systeme, 1929, p. 289 f.

105. Erkenntnis, V. 2, pp. 75-77.

106. An Examination of Logical Positivism, 1936, p. 200-226.

107. "The entire series of another person's experiences here consists in nothing else than a re-arrangement of my experiences and their elements" (op. cit., p. 186).

108. Philosophy of Science, Vol. 3, 4, 1936, 1937.

109. "Wenn-so" ("Theoria". Vol. XI, 1945, p. 88 f.)

110. See later, p. 132.

111. As Wright, however, correctly pointed out (Den logiska Empirismen, Helsingfors, 1943, p. 56), the terms "atomic sentence" and "elementary sentence" are not synonymous by definition. For most atomic sentences express a *plurality* of facts since from each of them several non-analytic sentences are derivable which constitute their logical contents.

112. The question of protocol-sentences was vividly discussed in the Vienna Circle. See Carnap, "Die physikalische Sprache als Universalsprache der Wissenschaft" (Erkenntnis, V. 2, 1931-32, p. 437 f.); reply by Neurath, "Protokollsaetze" (Erkenntnis, V. 3, p. 204 f.); counterreply by Carnap, "Ueber Protokollsaetze" (Erkenntnis, V. 3, p. 214 f.). Zilsel, "Bemer-

kungen zur Wissenschaftslogik" (Erk., V. 3, p. 413 f.); reply by Carnap, ibid., p. 177 f; Juhos, "kritische Bemerkungen zur Wissenschaftstheorie des Physikalismus" (Erk., V. 4, 1933-34, p. 397 f.). There is a critical exposition of the protocol-theories of the Vienna Circle in Petzaell, Zum Methodenproblem der Erkenntnisforschung (Goeteborgs Hoegskolas Arskrift, V. 41, 1935).

113. Schlick, Das Fundament der Erkenntnis (Erkenntnis, V. 4, 1934; Gesammelte Aufsaetze, p. 291).

114. Carnap, Erkenntnis, V. 2, p. 438.

115. Erkenntnis, V. 3, p. 209 f.

116. As Reininger already had maintained with respect to sense-statements (Metaphysik der Wirklichkeit, 1931, pp. 132-34).

117. "Any sentence of the systematic physical language is under circumstances qualified to serve as protocol sentence", says Carnap: "Ueber Protokollsaetze", Erkenntnis V. 3, p. 224.

118. Ibid.

119. Erkenntnis, V. 3, p. 209.

120. Erkenntnis, V. 4, 1934; Ges. Aufsaetze, p. 290 f.; cf. also Cornelius, Zur Kritik der wissenschaftlichen Grundbegriffe (Erkenntnis, V. 2, 1931, p. 206 f.)

121. The concept of "Konstatierung" has been defended and further elaborated by B. Juhos, "Negationsformen empirischer Saetze" (Erk., V. 6, 1936, p. 41 f.); "Empirische Saetze und logische Konstanten" (Journal of Unified Science, V. 8, p. 354 f.); "Principles of Logical Empiricism". (Mind, V. 46).

122. Schlick, Ges. Aufsaetze, p. 303, 309.

123. Radikaler Physikalismus und 'Wirkliche Welt' (Erkenntnis, V. 4, 1934, p. 346 f.)

124. Schriften zur wissenschaftlichen Weltauffassung, V. 9. Schlick was likewise criticized by Petzaell, in "Zum Methodenproblem der Erkenntnisforschung" (Goeteborgs Hoegskolas Arskrift, V. 41, 1935, p. 37 f.)

125. Das Fundament der Erkenntnis, in G.A., p. 304.

126. cf. Schlick, Positivismus und Realismus (Ges. Aufsaetze, p. 95, 96.)

127. Popper's position as regards determination by the empirically given is not unambiguous, though. On the one hand, he admits a "connection" between acceptable basic sentences and observation-sentences, but on the other hand one discerns a tendency in Popper to found confirmation exclusively on logical relations. In this way he slides from empiricism to conventionalism. He says with regard to basic sentences (loc. cit., p. 203): "We may interpret their acceptance as a conventional decision and the accepted sentences as conventions".

128. See also Carnap, Die logische Syntax der Sprache, p. 426.

129. This consideration is repeatedly urged by Weinberg (An Examination of Logical Positivism, 1936, p. 254, 255). But as Carnap has in the meantime abandoned the exclusively syntactic point of view and is now doing full justice to the semantic point of view, no difficulty remains

in this respect.
130. See later, p. 163 f.
131. Popper, Die Logik der Forschung, p. 188.
132. "Ueber das Fundament der Erkenntnis", *Ges. Aufsaetze*, p. 303. I myself examined in detail the inductive procedure from the logico-epistemological point of view, in my "Grundformen der wissenschaftlichen Methoden" (S.-B. d. Wiener Akademie der Wissenschaften, Phil.-hist. Kl., B. 203, 3. Abh., 1925).
133. If so, the concept of a truth-function also loses its fundamental significance for epistemology, since knowledge of empirical propositions cannot be analyzed into conjunctive knowledge of elementary propositions.
134. General Propositions and Causality, 1929 (reprinted in "The Foundations of Mathematics", New York 1931).
135. Die Kausalitaet in der gegenwaertigen Physik (Naturwissenschaften, 1931; Ges. Aufsaetze, p. 55 f.)
136. Felix Kaufmann, Das Unendliche in der Mathematik und seine Ausschaltung, 1930. See also the review by Carnap, in the Deutsche Literaturzeitung, 1930, Sp. 1674 f.
137. This view had been anticipated by Weyl; see "Die heutige Erkenntnislage in der Mathematik" (Symposium I, p. 19): "A universal judgment is not a genuine judgment but rather a precept for forming a judgment".
138. Carnap too refuses to recognize, in the *Aufbau*, unrestrictedly universal sentences as legitimate, and uses only molecular sentences, interpreting laws of nature as conjunctions of so far verified sentences about individual experiences from which they are induced (analogous to Mach's conception of laws as abbreviations for lists of such sentences).
139. "Ueber die All-Saetze" (Actes du 8e Congrès internat. de Philosophie à Prague 1934, 1936. p. 187 f.) Whether unrestrictedly universal statements are meaningful depends on whether the use of an unrestricted universal operator is meaningful, of an operator, that is, which refers to an unlimited totality instead of a limited totality admitting of conjunctive enumeration.
140. Testability and Meaning, Phil. of Science, V. 4, p. 24 f.
141. Carnap, Testability and Meaning, loc. cit., p. 26.
142. Testability and Meaning, Vol. III, p. 438.
143. cf. Poincaré, Science and Hypothesis (transl. J. Royce), p. 81.
144. Popper, Die Logik der Forschung, p. 42 f.
145. cf. V. Kraft, Mathematik, Logik und Erfahrung, 1947, p. 88 f.
146. See Popper, loc. cit., p. 80 f., and appendix I, p. 210 f.
147. Popper wants to reduce the principle of the uniformity of Nature to the methodological postulate of the spatial and temporal invariance of the laws of nature. He regards the mentioned principle as a "metaphysical misinterpretation of a methodological rule" (p. 187). According to him the postulate of invariance *defines* the concept of "law of nature". However, a methodological postulate and a definition are not

enough for natural knowledge. What is further needed is a proof of the existence of that which has been defined, the methodological postulate must be capable of being satisfied by the given. What the principle of the uniformity of Nature asserts is that such is actually the case.

148. cf. Carnap, Testability . . . , Vol. III, p. 425. Also Lewis, Experience and Meaning (Philos. Review, Vol. 43, 1934, p. 137, footnote 12) and Nagel, Verifiability, Truth and Verification (Journal of Philosophy. Vol. 31, 1934, p. 144 f.)

149. In Testability and Meaning, Vol. III, p. 431 f.

150. loc. cit., p. 203.

151. "Radikaler Physikalismus and 'wirkliche Welt'", Erkenntnis V. IV, 1934, p. 346 f.

152. "Remarks on Induction and Truth", Philosophy and Phenom. Research, Vol. 6, 1946, p. 590 f.

153. Extensive discussions about probability were held already at the first congress in Prague. See Erkenntnis, Vol. I, 1930/31, pp. 158-285.

154. As by Reichenbach, Wahrscheinlichkeitslehre, 1935 (Engl. translation 1949), earlier by R.v. Mises, Wahrscheinlichkeit, Statistik, Wahrheit, 1928, 2nd ed. 1936 (Engl. transl. 1939)

155. loc. cit., p. 188 f.

156. Carnap attempts at the present time to construct a formal concept of logical probability in analogy to mathematical probability; this construction, however, is entirely independent of the frequency theory. "On Inductive Logic" (Philosophy of Science, Vol. 12, 1945, p. 72. f.); "The Two Concepts of Probability" (Philosophy and Phenomenological Research, Vol. 5, 1945, p. 513 f.)

   In the meantime, Carnap has worked his theory of probability out in detail, in *Logical Foundations of Probability,* University of Chicago Press, 1950 (translator's note).

157. op. cit.

158. Wahrscheinlichkeit und Erfahrung, in *Erkenntnis,* V. I, p. 249 f.

159. Logische Analyse des Wahrscheinlichkeitsbegriffs, *Erkenntnis,* V. I, p. 228 f.

160. See Popper, op. cit., pp. 115, 116, 101.

161. *Erkenntnis,* Vol. I, p. 268, 269.

162. Ges. Aufsaetze, p. 73.

163. Logik der Forschung, p. 94 f.

164. *op. cit.,* p. 133.

165. Popper defines a chance event as an unpredictable event. The chance character of a series is, however, compatible with causal determination of the individual events constituting it.—This view is contrary to Schlick's (Ges. Aufsaetze, p. 72).

166. cf. Duerr, Die Einheit der Wissenschaften (*Erkenntnis,* Vol. 7, p. 65 f.)

167. cf. Carnap, Die physikalische Sprache als Universalsprache der Wissenschaft (*Erkenntnis,* Vol. II, p. 432 f..); Carnap, Psychologie in physikalischer Sprache (*Erkenntnis,* Vol. III, p. 107 f.); Neurath, Empirische

Soziologie, 1931 (Schriften z. Wissenschaftl. Weltauffassung, V. 5); Neurath, Physikalismus (Scientia, V. 50, 1931); Neurath, Einheitswissenschaft und Psychologie, 1933 (Einheitswissenschaft, Heft 1). It is the purpose of the Encyclopedia of Unified Science, edited by Carnap and Morris since 1938, to promote the ideal of unified science.‎

168. Testability and Meaning, Vol. 3, p. 466 f.
169. Die physikalische Sprache als Universalsprache der Wissenschaft (*Erkenntnis*, Vol. II, 1931. p. 445).
170. Psychologie in physikalischer Sprache (*Erkenntnis*, Vol. III, p. 108).
171. Die physikal. Sprache als Universalsprache d. Wissenschaft (loc. cit., p. 450).
172. *Erkenntnis*, Vol. II, pp. 456, 457.
173. *Erkenntnis*, Vol. III, p. 108.
174. An entirely analogous view is held by Kotarbinski, who calls it "reism". See R. Rand, "Kotarbinski's Philosophie", in *Erkenntnis*, Vol. 7, 1937-38, p. 97 f.
175. *Erkenntnis*, Vol. III,, p. 142.
176. *Erkenntnis*, Vol. III, p. 122, 124.
177. *Erkenntnis*, Vol. III p,. 136.
178. *Erkenntnis*, Vol. III, p. 458.
179. This line of criticism is taken among others by Dunker, in his article "Behaviorismus und Gastaltpsychologie" (*Erkenntnis*, Vol. III, p. 162 f.)
180. Erkenntnis, Vol. II, p. 459, 460.
181. Carnap, Scheinprobleme, p. 40.
182. See later, p. 177 f.
183. See earlier, p. 41 f.
184. Erkenntnis, Vol. II, p. 458.
185. Rougier used a similar argument, in "Le langage de la physique est-il universelle et autonome?", Erkenntnis, Vol. 7, 1937-38, p. 189 f.
186. As Carnap says, in "Psychologie in physikalischer Sprache", Erkenntnis, Vol. III, p. 126.
187. Objections against the physicalist language of unified science were raised also from another angle, by Kokoszynska, in "Bemerkungen ueber die Einheitswissenschaft" (Erkenntnis, Vol. 7, p. 325 f.) Not all scientific statements can be formulated in one and the same language, such as statements referring to truth, designation, definability in a given language. This objection, however, which is based exclusively on logical statements, loses its force if the thesis of the unity of scientific language applies only to *extra*-logical statements, as explained by Carnap (Logical Foundations of the Unity of Science, in Encyclopedia of Unified Science, Vol. I, No. 1). The only relevant question is whether all statements of *this* kind are reducible to physical statements. On the other hand, an ingenious attempt was made by Kaila to give a behavioristic analysis of the symbolizing function ("Physikalismus and Phaenomenalismus", *Theoria*, Vol. 8, 1942).
188. "The objects which are logically constructed out of perceptions do

not correspond to any external reality beyond the perceptions", says Ph. Frank (Erkenntnis, Vol. II, p. 186).

189. Erkenntnis, Vol. III, 1932; Ges. Aufsaetze, p. 83 f. (This essay has been translated into English, and commented upon, by David Rynin, in *Synthese*, Vol. VII, 1948-49, no. 6-B. Translator's note.)

190. Ges. Aufsaetze, p. 107, also p. 102.

191. Ibid., p. 352.

192. Ibid., p. 365.

193. Ibid., p. 115.

194. Ibid., p. 114; cf. note 187.

195. cf. Carnap, Scheinprobleme der Philosophie, 1928; Ph. Frank, Das Kausalgesetz, 1931 (Schriften zur wissenschaftlichen Weltauffassung, V. 6, ch. 10); Cornelius, Zur Kritik der wissenschaftl. Grundbegriffe (Erk., V. II, p. 191).

196. Carnap, Die logische Syntax der Sprache, p. 237; Scheinprobleme der Philosophie, 1928.

197. Ueberwindung der Metaphysik durch logische Analyse der Sprache (Erkenntnis, Vol. II, p. 237).

198. Likewise Ayer (Language, Truth and Logic, 1936, Ch. 6) interprets value judgments, not as assertions, but as expressions of feelings.

199. See V. Kraft, Grundlagen einer wissenschaftlichen Wertlehre, 1937 (Schriften zur wissenschaftl. Weltauffassung, V. 4).

200. Fragen der Ethik, 1930 (Schriften z. wissenschaftl. Weltauffassung, V. 4); English translation ("Problems of Ethics") by D. Rynin, 1939.

201. op. cit., p. 95 f.

202. loc. cit., p. 24 f. Almost simultaneously Joergensen maintained the analogous distinction for imperatives (norms): Imperatives and **Logic**, in *Erkenntnis,* Vol. 7, 1937-38, p. 288.

203. The same point is made by Joergensen, Imperatives and Logic (loc. cit.,) and by Rose Rand, Die Logik der Forderungssaetze (Internat. Zeitschrift f. Theorie d. Rechts, 1939).

204. In contrast to Joergensen's view (loc. cit.) — if "meaning", that is, is not restricted to descriptive meaning.

205. For this reason some radicals in the Vienna Circle, primarily Neurath, but likewise Carnap (in the "Logical Syntax of Language", p. 205, 206), were not disinclined to abandon altogether the term "philosophy" and even "theory of knowledge". Schlick, however, protested against this recommendation, in his essay "L'école de Vienne et la philosophie traditionelle" (Ges. Aufsaetze, p. 391 f.).

206. Die Wende der Philosophie, Ges. Aufsaetze, p. 31 f.

207. Die Wende der Philosophie, loc. cit., p. 36; also in Erk., V. I, 1930-31, p. 8.

208. Die logische Syntax der Sprache, p. 252.

209. See Erkenntnis, Vol. II, p. 91 f.

210. See Erkenntnis, Vol. 5, p. 56 f., p. 178 f.

211. Schlick, Die Kausalitaet in der gegenwaertigen Physik (Ges. Aufsaetze,

p. 41 f.; also in "Gesetz, Kausalitaet und Wahrscheinlichkeit", Wien 1948); Frank, Das Kausalgesetz und seine Grenzen, 1932 (Schr. z. wissenschaftl. W. auff., V. 6); see also the congress in Kopenhagen, 1936, in Erk., V. 6, p. 293 f.

212. Schlick, Ges. Aufsaetze, p. 251 f.

213. cf. Windelband, Lehrbuch der Geschichte der Philosophie, ed. v. Heimsoeth, 1935, p. 3: "This self-confident attitude of philosophy was shaken by Kant who demonstrated the impossibility of 'philosophical' (metaphysical) knowledge of the world besides or above the knowledge gained in the special sciences. After this renunciation, the domain of philosophy as a special discipline was narrowed down to just that critical self-consciousness of reason".

INDEX OF PROPER NAMES

208

INDEX OF PROPPER NAMES